JERRY A
DICTIONARY

JERRY ATTRICK'S DICTIONARY

Modern Words for Old-fashioned New Zealanders

Lew Goodman

REED

Published by Reed Books, a division of Reed Publishing (NZ) Ltd,
39 Rawene Rd, Birkenhead, Auckland. Website www.reed.co.nz.
Associated companies, branches and representatives throughout
the world.

This book is copyright. Except for the purpose of fair reviewing,
no part of this publication may be reproduced or transmitted in
any form or by any means, electronic or mechanical, including
photocopying, recording, or any information storage and
retrieval system, without permission in writing from the publisher.
Infringers of copyright render themselves liable to prosecution.

ISBN 0 7900 0695 2

© 1999 Lew Goodman

The author asserts his moral rights in the work.

Cover and text designed by Jerry Rota
Illustrations by Nobby Clark

First published 1999

Printed in Hong Kong

Preface

The speed of modern life leaves the senior citizen spinning in its wake. Long-held memories become clouded, or grossly embellished, and it is hoped that this compilation may enable some to recall 'the good old days'. I have relied heavily on personal experience and observation. I hope the reader finds these definitions of some use, and that the dictionary increases their understanding of some of today's language.

The vocabulary used by ordinary New Zealanders has changed almost beyond recognition; for example, many foreign words have come into common usage. Words such as garlic, olive oil, pasta, cappuccino and soy sauce were unheard of in the 1950s. Just imagine asking your sweetheart out for a cappuccino. She would have beaten you around the head with her handbag and strangled you with the sleeve of her cardigan, leaving you bruised and bewildered, before running home to her mother to complain about the unnatural demands you had made of her.

With the aid of this book, 'with it' geriatrics should be able to gain an insight into the new meanings of old words and use them in meaningful conversation with people of all ages.

If all else fails, remind your disrespectful family, friends and acquaintances that grannies and granddads rule the world and if anyone argues with you, you'll change your will.

Lew Goodman

A? Sometimes written EH? Used frequently prior to an appointment with an audiologist. Also used by the young when asked to set the table or identify a butter knife; also when one begins to reminisce about Greta Garbo or the Western Desert.

ABRASION A wound such as that received in the supermarket when one is rammed in the shins by a trolley steered by an out-of-control CHILD. Also what its parent threatens you with if you complain.

ABSENT-MINDED When one's mind goes on holiday without its owner buying the tickets.

ACCIDENT An occurrence, usually on the road, which is always the fault of an older person, never that of the young hoon travelling through a red light at 150 kph, hitting your car in the process. Often accompanied by the words, 'You shouldn't be on the road, granddad.'

ACQUISITIONS The valued belongings which one painstakingly collects during one's lifetime and lovingly cares for in old age. When you pass on, your relatives either squabble over who gets what, or take them all to the nearest dump.

ADDRESS The place where you live but are never able to remember when you are asked to write it on the back of a cheque. This inability causes suspicion among (usually young) shop assistants, who do not understand this syndrome and adopt the 'stolen cheque book' look.

AEROPLANE A cramped flying machine that the airlines deliberately overbook, before sifting out the elderly passengers by making boarding announcements in unintelligible whispers. See also CHILD.

AFFLICTION Common in the elderly, a term used to describe everything from piles, to the inability to hold one's glass steady, to (on a bad day) one's children.

AGE A term used to describe the time between birth and now. See also AGEING, AGELESS.

AGEING Depending on the speaker, used either to describe the process of becoming wise, tolerant and even more lovable, or doddering, frustrating and past it.

AGELESS A term used to describe an infuriating person, frequently a woman, who refuses to exhibit the usual (negative) signs of AGEING.

AGILITY Once meant the capacity to run like a hare; now refers to the ability to flex one's big toe while seated.

AH!

AH! A useful word that can be used to express a variety of emotions:
1. The frustration of trying to persuade your body to take up the position necessary to enter your daughter's Honda City;
2. The pain of hitting your thumb with a hammer because you are wearing the wrong glasses;
3. The relief of sitting down quietly in your favourite chair after seeing your beloved family out of the door;
4. The nostalgic mixture of pleasure and regret evoked by remembering Clark Gable kissing Vivien Leigh.

AGELESS

Ailment

AILMENT A term used to describe a painful or debilitating illness for which there is no known cure, to the frustration of the sufferer and the delight of the medical profession. Common in the elderly.

AJAR Used mainly by the elderly to describe the partial opening of a door or window, usually by a young person, thus creating an irritating draught.

AKIN Related to or next to; for example, my teeth should be akin my bed.

ALTERCATION A brief, noisy argument with the neighbours, generally in response to the nocturnal habits of their cats and their association with your newly planted flower beds. This term usually appears in police reports on such incidents.

AMAZING Another word much used by the elderly. Can be applied to a range of phenomena such as one's grandchildren's clothing and hairstyles, inventions such as the automatic washing machine and the computer, or the latest crop of television weather presenters; also frequently heard in connection with the previous night's episode of 'Baywatch'.

ANTICLIMAX When personal expectations fail to be fulfilled; for example, during sex.

AOTEAROA A country, also known as New Zealand. Increasingly used by television personalities and some

Astute

politicians, causing confusion among the elderly, some of whom believe it to be a new brand of thermal underwear.

APPLICATION
A word whose meaning changes with time.
1. To the young it is a word that evokes hope and anticipation; for example, filling in a job or passport application. To the elderly it has more sinister overtones, and is often used in the sense of filling in an application for surgery, a pension, or an extension of time for rates payment.
2. A smearing of medication or ointment, which is generally unpleasantly greasy and odorous, making one's family sniff and regard one suspiciously.
3. An obsolete term meaning what one brought to one's study or employment; something akin to dedication. This meaning is rarely heard today and in the young frequently elicits the response 'EH?' See also A/EH?

ARTHRITIS A painful disease described by Humphrey Bogart in the film 'Casablanca' with the memorable words, 'This is a swell joint.' See also HIP.

ASTUTE This term refers to the elderly who still have money invested or saved, despite raising three children, owning a house and making frequent interest-free loans to anyone who shares their surname.

Atomiser

ATOMISER A device for creating fine mists that are absorbed through bodily orifices, principally the nose. Also used to describe US President Truman.

AUDIOLOGY A science which enables people to hear things they would rather not hear.

AVOIDANCE A legitimate activity in the elderly, who do not usually associate it with tax. It is more commonly used to refer to the act of swerving around things when one is driving one's electric carriage, or changing direction rapidly when one sees a small, noisy CHILD coming toward one (or the neighbour with whom one had the embarrassing ALTERCATION the previous day).

AWAKE The state in which many elderly people pass their nights (the opposite of somnolent, the state in which many spend a large part of their afternoons). Can be associated with the prostate gland, in which case also with frequent exercise, as most elderly cannot afford an en suite. See also ARTHRITIS.

AXIOM A thing you once thought was true and worthwhile, but now most commonly classified as 'old-fashioned', which puts one in one's place. See also A/EH?

AYE Still commonly used by those of Scottish persuasion, even those who emigrated over fifty years ago. Loosely translated, it means 'yes'.

AZURE The colour of some eyes prior to the formation of those nasty white rings around the iris.

B

BACKACHE A curious AILMENT which prevents sufferers from helping family members move furniture and perform physical work. It is often intermittent, and in young men is generally most severe on Saturdays during the rugby season.

BAD BREATH A condition of which the sufferer is not always aware. Often diagnosed by one's younger grandchildren, who identify it with the colloquial term 'Yuk'.

BALDERDASH A collective term used by the elderly in response to any ideas with which they disagree; most commonly applied when addressing a member of the younger generation. (A reciprocal term, used by the young in response to any idea expressed by their elders, might be 'Get real.')

BALDNESS A genetic disorder which passes down the male line from father to son. It is often a source of humour (unappreciated by the sufferer) and less commonly regarded as a sign of sex appeal, though rarely in the elderly.

Battery

BATTERY A modern invention used to power vital tools such as hearing aids, pacemakers and transistor radios. The former are often infuriatingly small and impossible to pick up; the latter are usually flat.

BED An apparatus for sleeping on. Usually full of lumps and misplaced springs; often too high, wide, narrow, hot, cold, squeaky and generally, no matter how expensive, uncomfortable.

The elderly are often heard to express a preference for their own bed (in contrast to the young, who often prefer other people's), but this is something of an irrelevance as most elderly do the majority of their sleeping in comfortable chairs at odd times during the day. See also AWAKE.

BEER A brown liquid, generally regarded as an essential accompaniment to watching games of rugby and cricket, particularly on television. Traditionally a male drink (see also BELCH), it is increasingly being consumed by females, to the consternation of males who worry about a shortage of supplies.

BEER BELLY See BULGE.

BELCH A rapid expulsion of stomach gas, mostly air, which often occurs without warning. Young men often use the belch as an expression of their manhood after drinking copius amounts of BEER; in the elderly it is likely to elicit the response 'Dad!' in one's children, and uncontrollable giggles in one's grandchildren.

BIB An essential item of clothing in the very young and the very old. The bib is tied around the neck and hangs down over the chest and upper abdomen, where it catches pieces of food that drop from the mouth through the gaps left by missing teeth. The food can then be retrieved from the bib and a second attempt made to put it in the mouth.

BLOOD A red fluid that circulates round the body. Blood varies according to age, season and genetics; it may be thin, thick, watery or simply bad.

BODY The misshapen part of a person which is not mind.

BONES Internal body structures on which hang vital organs. They tend to warp as a result of increasing weight being placed on them, and the process of AGE-ING, often developing a mind of their own. Some bones, such as those in the legs and arms, become more obvious as one ages and the flesh hangs from them rather than covering them appealingly; these should be covered at all times in public to avoid offending the young.

BOREDOM A condition of the mind often brought on by being forced to listen to one's friends' stories day after day, year after year. It is the nature of boredom that the inducer is generally unable to detect the condition.

BOWELS A part of the digestive system that is often a source of embarrassment to its owner and fascination to the nursing profession. Bowels may be open, but never

Bowls

shut; working, but never unemployed; loose, but never tight. Overworking bowels cause their owner to remain indoors, preferably in their own home, where they are familiar with the plumbing system necessary to cope with this problem.

BOWLS A popular game among the elderly, which can be played in singles, pairs or fours. Men are attracted to bowling clubs because of the ready availability of cheap beer; despite this, women often encourage their menfolk to join as it gets them out of the house (i.e. out from under their feet). Inappropriate behaviour between male and female players is discouraged by the thoughtfully designed uniforms, which make the women look like dental nurses of the old school, and the men like out-of-work cricketers.

BOWLS

Bulge

BRAIN A soft organ in the head which appears to reduce in size with age, making it difficult to remember what it was like in the first place.

BRAN A cereal once fed mainly to horses, now fashionable among the elderly, who are said to need it to provide 'roughage'. This term aptly describes the texture of bran; eating it is similar to eating a sandwich on a windy beach.

BRIERLEY, SIR RON Ex-New Zealander regarded by many elderly as a demi-god. Gives guest appearances at BIL shareholders' meetings, where he is invariably greeted by the chant 'Bring back Ron, bring back Ron,' and is mobbed by blue-haired ladies who would love to take him home and give him a good feed. See also CRASH.

BROKE A common condition of the elderly, meaning to have little or no money. Special government departments are devoted to ensuring the maintenance of this condition among the elderly, even if they are still in the workforce. One of their activities is best known as asset stripping.

BULGE A swelling, common in the abdomen, due to loss of muscle tone. A frequent misconception is that bulges are formed as a result of consuming excessive quantities of food and/or drink (see BEER), with subsequent deposits of fat.

Bunion

BUNION A type of spare toe which grows out from the side of the foot. Bunions are easier to maintain than the natural toe because they have no nails which require cutting. One disadvantage of bunions is that to accommodate them you need to buy shoes which are several sizes larger than normally required. This may cause you to trip over frequently, a problem that is dealt with elsewhere — generally in casualty departments, if you can find one. Although bunions can be a source of pain to the elderly, to the young they are more often a source of amusement.

BUS A form of transport which sometimes runs on time but never when it is raining. The queues that are formed by those waiting for buses can be useful for those who want a rest in hospital; make sure you are well up in the queue and you stand a good chance of being pushed over on the steps, which can lead to breaking the neck or the thigh bone.

BUTTOCKS That portion of the body which bears its weight when a person is seated. Buttocks are sometimes described as buxom, full, rounded and shapely, although these terms are generally reserved for the young. With time the buttocks have a tendency to expand, shrivel, or simply droop, and in the elderly they are most frequently referred to as skinny, fat or, by the younger generation, 'gross'.

CACKLE A type of laugh particularly associated with the elderly, especially those who have missing front teeth and facial warts. It is well worth perfecting the art of the cackle, which can be used to terrify the young, and can be a great asset when babysitting.

CALL A communication, especially by telephone. A call usually occurs when one is otherwise engaged, generally at the greatest possible distance from the telephone. Hastening to answer can leave you so breathless you are unable to make any contribution to the conversation; this may give the caller the impression that you no longer wish to talk to them, with the result that they may snub you at the next social gathering you both attend. See TELEPHONE.

CALLERS People who CALL, either on the telephone or in person, when their reception may vary according to the types and quantity of cakes they bring with them for afternoon tea, whether they are accompanied by a CHILD or children, and whether they are in pairs bearing religious tracts. The latter frequently attempt to gain favour with the elderly by bewailing the morals and

Calm

demeanour of the younger generation, a ploy which frequently backfires, causing the elderly callee to remember with great affection their favourite child or grandchild.

CALM Used to describe one's attitude when all the senses have shut down because there is nothing worthwhile happening. Also the feeling one gets when the last of the family have left after a prolonged Christmas visit.

CALORIES An invention that has come to us from the US, understood and valued only by those people who have made a science out of counting them. Notwithstanding the general public's bewilderment over and indifference to calories, the science of counting them has spread widely and is now well entrenched in New Zealand.

Some 64,942 New Zealanders are employed full time in counting calories, making this the country's second largest occupational group, next to public hospital administrators.

CAMPHOR A substance used (a) to protect woollen clothes from the ravages of moths, and (b) to keep others at a distance, the effect of the volatile fumes produced when one is dressed in clothing that has been so treated. Also used as an oil, which is rubbed on the chest to avoid congestion, and doubling as an insect repellent during the summer season. Camphor is only ever used by the elderly; the young (a) do not understand the work of moths and regard holes in clothes as a fashion statement, and (b) have developed their own highly effective, and much more menacing, methods of keeping other people at a distance.

CANARY A small bird with a beautiful song. Canaries provide pleasure and companionship out of all proportion to the minimal cost of keeping them — a handful of seed and a small amount of green vegetation seem small compensation for the enjoyment they give. Cats also enjoy these birds, and perhaps provide companionship for them, as they can frequently be found circling their cages and gazing longingly at their occupants.

CAN'T A word seldom used by the elderly, most of whom remember wars, the Depression and many other adversities, all of which they class as character-building, particularly when talking to those who have not experienced these events and probably never will.

CANTANKEROUS Quarrelsome, niggly, argumentative and bullish. This condition is seldom admitted to by the sufferer, who instantly becomes aggressive when accused of it, thus proving the diagnosis.

CAP An article of clothing worn by those of English persuasion, but now not uncommon in New Zealand. Worn on the head, it was once used to denote membership of the Trades Union Society, but now indicates that the wearer is a stockbroker or lawyer, with a twelve handicap in golf. A Dutch cap is a different article altogether, and is not a cap worn by Dutchmen.

Capable

CAP

CAPABLE Able to do things successfully. Frequently used in sentences such as 'I am not doing his washing, he is quite capable of doing it himself.'

CAPTIVATING A word never used to describe the elderly.

CARE To take care means never crossing the road, even in broad daylight.

CAREGIVER A modern term used to describe some of life's treasures; for example, home helps, district nurses and meals-on-wheels drivers. The term can also be applied, erroneously, to those who attempt to control one's life by doing irritating things such as helping one write out cheques and making inedible pots of stew. These 'caregivers' are often family members.

CHILD
1. Affectionate progeny of one's offspring whose visits (a) turn one's house upside down and raise one's blood pressure, and (b) make life worth living.

2. Unrelated progeny who precipitate painful accidents in the supermarket (see ABRASION) and cause mild panic when found near one in an AEROPLANE or other confined space; known to be noisy, frequently smelly, and embarrassingly frank.

CHIROPODY Care of the feet. This includes removal of calluses, corns, excess nail growth and other abnormalities which cause pain. The feeling after treatment has been described as like walking on air, but this only lasts until you replace your shoes.

CHRONIC A term often used with AILMENT, referring to an illness that persists for many years. Chronic ailments are more expensive than other ailments because they tend to involve repeated visits to so-called 'specialists', who are generally unable, despite their title, to relieve the condition.

CIRCULATION The movement of blood through a series of pipes in the body, propelled by a single pump called the heart. It can be annoying when the system fails, as this may result in permanent damage, called death. Circulation can be improved by jogging, especially if the joggers are young, with supple, bouncing, muscular bodies. In fact, just imagining this has already improved my circulation.

CIVIL The art of being polite to those with whom you have nothing in common. The habit of giving your true opinion will quickly earn you the label 'uncivil'.

Clean

CLEAN A pronouncement made by your family only after an exhaustive examination of your shirt collar, jersey front, fingernails and those hard-to-shave places which you might have missed that morning.

CLOTHES Your wardrobe, generally made up of articles made from natural fibres which are more comfortable than fashionable. Most of these you will have owned for many years, some even having been handed on from your parents. Often the subject of derision and even mirth among your family, they can be adjudged to have returned to fashionable status when one of your teenage grandchildren asks to borrow an item to wear to a school dance.

CLUTTER Your cultural display of furniture, china and knick-knacks, painstakingly and lovingly accumulated over many years. Often given the term clutter by visitors, particularly family members, when they find there is no clear space in which to place their cup of tea, or when a CHILD has knocked one of your most prized pieces to the floor.

COFFEE A pleasant drink that should not be consumed prior to retiring, as it contains a stimulant which may keep the consumer awake and, if strong enough, lead to other nocturnal activities which are not considered appropriate in the elderly.

Some ladies participate in coffee mornings, at which they discuss other ladies who are unable or unwilling to attend.

COHERENT Refers to the ability to talk without rambling, making oneself clearly understood by one's listeners. Members of Parliament and the clergy are rarely coherent, and the quality is in scarce supply in the pensions section of the Social Welfare Department, whose employees are highly trained in the art of incoherent speech. The young often hold the view that the elderly are rarely coherent; the elderly hold a similar view of the young, particularly those in their teens.

COLLYWOBBLES A condition observed immediately prior to the opening of a power bill.

COMMODE An apparatus which closely resembles a pipe frame fitted with a toilet seat. I have no idea what it is for, and can only guess that it is designed with the express purpose of causing the maximum discomfort to those unfortunate enough to be forced to sit on it. The more 'comfortable' types are manufactured from wood.

CONDENSE To make smaller. The elderly often become condensed as they age. An extreme example of this is a two-metre (six foot six) tall basketball player, famous in the 1930s, who is now a height-diminished person touring the world with the Snow White show. Very old people may disappear entirely.

CONSCIOUS The state of being aware. This is not always a positive attribute, particularly when it means being able to hear derogatory remarks made by others as you

Conversation

enter a room or board a bus; however, unconsciousness can always be feigned. This is particularly useful when hospital visitors, or your family, discuss you as if you were not present, or when they stay too long and you begin to suffer extreme BOREDOM.

CONVERSATION The art of making oneself heard by speaking louder than everyone else. Many conversations are very short, but they are appreciated by the hard of hearing.

COORDINATION The ability to get one's muscles to move in the correct sequence, so that the left leg passes the right leg when walking. Poor coordination can cause the loss of friends, as you tend to drop and break things they treasure. Such items are usually family heirlooms, some of them many hundreds of years old, and generally irreplaceable.

CORN A yellow vegetable which is often considered a delicacy, but which is very difficult to eat with either false or few teeth. When served at barbecues it can easily be smuggled away without offending one's host, but it is more difficult to deal with in a formal dining situation. This causes few problems for the elderly, however, who are generally considered inappropriate guests on these occasions.

The word corn is also used to describe painfully thickened skin on the toes and feet, which is sometimes caused by buying op shop shoes. See CHIROPODY.

Cystoscope

CRAMP An interesting affliction which often occurs in the elderly, causing them to leap about and give a gymnastic display worthy of a medal at the Olympics. Not to be confused with AGILITY.

CRANK A person who does not fit the definition of 'normal' (a word that itself defies definition). Most collectors are cranks; for example, the Wanganui collector who has four thousand burnt-out light bulbs in his candlelit home. Many elderly people are regarded as cranks, but this is because they have long since realised that striving to be 'normal' is fruitless and boring. See ECCENTRIC, NUTTY.

CRASH A word that came to prominence in 1987, and which should never be used within the hearing of those holding large blocks of BRIERLEY shares.

CROCHET A form of HANDICRAFT done by dextrous ladies who throughout winter manufacture items such as milk jug covers while watching 'Neighbours' on television. These items are sold at church fairs, and bought by faithful members of the congregation who have not the faintest idea what to do with them.

CYSTOSCOPE A surgical instrument designed by Attila the Hun and still used by surgeons (who have modified it by increasing its diameter to cause maximum after-pain) to examine unmentionable parts of the body. Mention of this word in the RSA bar causes patrons to start drinking double whiskies.

DAB Mainly used in the expression 'dab hand', meaning a person who has a special skill which can be exploited by family and friends. Possibly the worst dab-hand skill to have is that of house painting and decorating, for obvious reasons. Fortunately, most elderly are not considered by younger members of their families to retain any dab-handedness.

DANCE A form of rhythmic movement during which the male partner firmly grips the female partner in close contact. Formerly most self-respecting males considered themselves to be threats to Fred Astaire, a name which today elicits the response EH? in the young, accompanied by glazed looks. The reality was that many women suffered permanent foot damage as a result of having their in-steps trodden on heavily by their partners. Modern dance has overcome this by not allowing partners to come within several metres of each other, thus avoiding foot damage and the clashing of heads.

DAPPER Male dancers were sometimes described as dapper, depending on their manner of dress. In larger families, the dapper member was often the one who

Debonair

could borrow the best clothes from his brothers. A long white silk scarf was an essential accessory, without which the term dapper could never be applied.

DARBY AND JOAN According to legend, two people who remained married for nearly one hundred years (or so it seemed) without murdering each other.

DEAD The state of being un-alive. A permanent condition when AGE ends.

DEBONAIR An anachronistic term applied to a man who is always well groomed, complete with brilliantined hair and lavender aftershave, and who is the envy of other males because he is the favourite among the ladies, joining them and conversing freely. Often seen at

DARBY AND JOAN

club dances and end-of-year presentations, etc. Other males may describe him in other ways, none of which refer to his grooming or manner, or are complimentary.

DEBT A lifelong consideration for most people, but less likely to be seen in the elderly, mainly because they consider themselves too old to spend time in Mt Eden, especially in the winter months.

DENTAL CARE Dental care is placed in the hands of dentists, who charge vast amounts to scrape, drill, fill, extract and polish teeth, only to replace them with plastic sets when they eventually fall out. Plastic teeth are a frequent source of annoyance to their owners, but this does not prevent some people from displaying them by flicking the lower denture out for public cleansing and to remove irritating items such as pips. This behaviour could be regarded as a show of wealth because of the gigantic cost of the teeth, but more often causes embarrassment and derision among the assembled company.

DEPRESSION A condition which is common in the elderly, and which can be quite serious if not treated. Not to be confused with the Depression, mention of which causes the young to yawn and rapidly leave the room. Many things cause depression, and short depressive states are often induced by having to attend family gatherings, such as your aunt's ninetieth birthday, where you know you will meet all your unloved and unlovable cousins, whom you have despised since the day they removed your worm collection from the jam jar in which

Digest

it was housed. This type of depression is treated relatively easily by taking several large doses of an alcoholic drink, although too much medication can cause it to return the following morning.

DESCEND In the elderly this often means to come down the stairs (or off the bus) rapidly by falling. Many New Zealand houses now have stairs, and the incidence of descending has shown a marked increase in recent years. It can cause DEPRESSION.

DIAGNOSIS A doctor's guess. Made after a consultation which often does not include discussion of your ailment, but consists mainly of a comparison of golf handicaps. More expensive diagnoses are made with the aid of extremely intricate machines in places that used to be, and are now once again, known as hospitals. Neither the hospitals nor the diagnoses are particularly appropriate for the elderly, because they can lead to possible further costly treatment and surgery. There is also the risk that by the time it is your turn you will no longer be alive.

DIGEST
1. The ability to eat and absorb all types of food and drink. Some elderly people still believe they can consume steak and eggs for breakfast, a couple of pies for lunch, and one of those great roasts for tea 'that only Mum can cook'. And most of us do, with the aid of a few litres of Mylanta and copious draughts of bicarbonate solution.

Dignity

2. As in Reader's Digest, a small magazine that used to be found in large piles in the outside dunny, and which kept Dad entertained when he disappeared in there for several hours after breakfast.

DIGNITY A state of poise and respect, rare in the young, and increasingly difficult to maintain as one declines into old age. Dignity ensures that you make an uncompromising impression by maintaining a straight back, talking in soft tones, and pretending that it is of no consequence when you are told that your fly is open or your shirt is hanging out. Maintaining one's dignity takes a lot of concentration and can be extremely tiring.

DISPENSARY Previously a shop filled with bottles from which elderly, wise people made up mixtures to cure all ailments. Some of the better ones had up to thirty bottles from which they could choose ingredients for their mixtures, nearly all of which were effective, but which were often foul tasting. Today's dispensaries are called pharmacies. These are mainly for the distribution of insect repellents, lipstick, nail polish and boxes of pills marked 'CAUTION' in red lettering, which have been imported from America and Europe.

DISTILLER The title given to those who play a most important part in society. Distillers' products are renowned for their mood-changing properties, and are often used during celebrations such as birthdays, Christmas, etc., during which they may cause the infirm

Doze

to dance, the unmusical to sing, and the old and cynical to experience feelings not experienced since their second day in school, when they realised they were completely infatuated with their teacher. Their use can be followed by a 'hangover', but I have never been able to discover how a town in Germany has any bearing on this subject.

DOG A canine animal, often kept as a pet. It may be regarded as a companion or as a pest, depending on your point of view. If you are its owner, it is a companion. If you live next door to its owner, it may be regarded as a pest. Many dog owners disregard the fact that their pet is a carnivore and will enjoy eating flesh, including that of the meter reader or any other unwary person foolish enough to call. Callers who are attacked and complain about the loss of flesh and blood they have suffered are often humiliated further by being told, 'My little Ripper would never bite. You must be mistaken.' A slammed door generally ends such conversations, although they sometimes continue in court. A dog's habit of barking is often overlooked by its owner, who frequently seems to suffer from selective nocturnal deafness.

DOZE A pleasant state in which the mind is allowed to roam at will. This condition is often seen in elderly men when their wives have invited lady friends for afternoon tea. Dozing in these situations may result in severe repercussions after the departure of the guests, and may be interrupted by a loud and unwelcome noise such as

Dwell

'WAKE UP AND GET OUT OF THAT CHAIR, THE LAWNS NEED MOWING.' See also NAP.

DWELL To remain with the mind or speech fixed on a subject. In the elderly, often seen in the form of dwelling on the past. This type of dwelling — which is usually discouraged by one's offspring — often causes falsification of past memories, many of which have become distorted or embellished. When dwelling on the past, the elderly often recall 'the good old days', forgetting the five-mile walk to school, having to boil the copper on wash day, and having to attend Sunday school, not to mention floor-scrubbing, range-stoking, etc. A classic example of this type of dwelling involves recalling the good times when families were not fragmented and people enjoyed themselves without relying solely on money.

EARS The organs of hearing, positioned on either side of the head. The ears are highly sophisticated pieces of equipment, with which the experienced owner can train himself (less commonly herself) to control reception and hear at will. This ability first manifests itself during early attendance at school, and is honed during many years of 'listening' to political speeches and television programmes. An expression frequently used to describe this ability is 'cloth ears'; most husbands develop cloth ears at various times during their lives. Other expressions that are used to describe ears include wingnuts, flaps, wings, Dumbos and pikelets.

ECCENTRIC Many elderly people are given this label, generally because they do not fit into modern patterns of accepted behaviour. Reasons for being labelled eccentric include wearing zip-up tartan slippers, not wearing coordinated clothing, painting one's house white, eating food such as tripe and onions, carrying an umbrella and, perhaps the defining factor, enjoying Richard Dawson, Guy Lombardo (who?) and 'Danny Boy'. See also CRANK, NUTTY.

Economy

ECONOMY The management of assets. It includes not wasting bread or other food, or money. The concept of economy is one that the younger generation find difficult to grasp, and it can cause friction among close family members. Insisting that superfluous lights are turned off invariably alienates the grandchildren, most of whom have mastered the skill of pulling the switch down, but have never worked out how to push it up. You may find yourself labelled ECCENTRIC simply because you do not choose to live in a home which is illuminated so that it resembles Disneyland on New Year's Eve.

ECSTASY Another concept never associated with the elderly.

EH? See A?

ELECTRICITY An energy source which is clean, efficient and cheap, until the bill arrives. The sudden failure of electricity can necessitate significant behavioural changes, and creates demand for the services of the elderly, who find themselves required to give demonstrations of fire lighting, producing and explaining the workings of candles, etc.

ELOPE To run off with and marry one's beloved without parental permission. Eloping is rare in today's world, mainly because marriage is no longer in fashion and 'parental permission' is an unknown term. When an elopement does occur, today's parents are inclined to greet the news with relief, knowing they will not have to

Embrace

shell out the cost of a large wedding, and that there will be one less member of the family to accommodate and feed. See EMPTY NEST SYNDROME.

EMANCIPATION Generally applied to women, and considered by men to be the most destructive policy ever introduced. The emancipation of women means that men are now expected to do a share of the housework, women have their own cheque books and – a recent and even more frightening development – credit cards, and do not consider it necessary to consult their husbands on where they go or who they invite into their houses. Giving women the vote was a major source of concern to men, a concern that has become even greater with the increasing numbers of women becoming Members of Parliament.

EMBALMING The preservation of the body after death, the purpose of which remains obscure. Most people rarely wish to view their relatives when they are alive, making it most unlikely they will wish to do so five years after their death. A notable exception is to be found in Red Square, Moscow.

EMBRACE To encircle or grip others with the arms. Many young males show a great desire to embrace young females, but often find themselves more likely to be embraced by members of the police force. Today embraces are seen frequently on television, particularly between soccer players, presidents (generally between males only; male presidents prefer to embrace females

Empty nest syndrome

in private) and young female members of the British royal family and (young) victims of illness and tragedy. The elderly welcome embraces, especially from grandchildren who are clean-shaven.

EMPTY NEST SYNDROME A syndrome in which women who had devoted themselves to their families suffered feelings of loss and inadequacy when their children left home. These symptoms were often temporarily relieved when the children occasionally returned (generally without warning) bearing bags of dirty washing and expecting to be fed. The syndrome is rare today, when women actively encourage their children to leave home as soon as possible so that they can concentrate on their own high-powered jobs (see EMANCIPATION). Some women (and even more men) look back longingly to the days of the empty nest syndrome when they find that their children are still firmly wedded to the comforts of home even in their late twenties.

ENERGY A quality to be treasured; often in irritatingly short supply in the elderly. Physical energy varies in intensity, particularly with the seasons. In winter many elderly partake of a form of hibernation in which they reduce their energy output, limiting it to stoking fires and making hot drinks. Other more robust types persist in believing they are potential Olympic champions, running the mile in less than twenty-seven minutes and being absolutely useless for other activities for the next twenty-four hours.

EQUITY The amount you thought you had invested in

Etiquette

your property until you got the lawyers' cheque following its sale.

ESSENTIAL Applied to articles which cannot be dispensed with, which tend to increase in number as one ages. These are often items that are required for personal use; for example, spectacles, teeth, walking sticks. Occasionally applied to close companions and family members. The loss of any essential item causes extreme stress and may cause recessive behaviour such as thumb-sucking or teddy-cuddling on retiring.

ETIQUETTE An established code of behaviour which lifts humans above animals. No longer applicable in modern society, but often practised by the elderly in the secrecy of their homes and clubs.

ETIQUETTE

Eulogy

EULOGY A speech made at the end of a function or life. Often drawn out and frequently lacking facts, a eulogy informs listeners of the subject's many positive attributes, most of which they were totally unaware of. Some members of the clergy have set eulogies for funerals, simply changing the names of the departed as necessary. This is somewhat risky if the subject is elderly, as it is likely many of the equally elderly listeners will hear the eulogy more than once within a short time frame. (But see EARS, particularly 'cloth ears'.)

EXERCISE Physical movement of the body or parts thereof. 'Regular exercise' is frequently prescribed by doctors, who are generally seated in comfortable chairs and give the impression of having no personal experience of this activity themselves.

The intensity and duration of exercise varies greatly according to personal preference, ranging from running marathons, climbing mountains and swimming oceans to the movement of the index finger while changing the television channel. The common expression 'Use it or lose it' inspires heated debate. Some people believe that overuse causes rapid wear and subsequent loss of the body part in question, and in consequence attempt to preserve their limbs and organs by doing absolutely nothing.

EXORBITANT As in 'That's an exorbitant amount to pay for a drink/taxi ride/(frequently) dress/MP's salary.'
See also EXCESSIVE.

Extravagant

EXCESSIVE A word that is frequently used by the elderly to describe present-day costs. Some older people have not yet grasped the currency changes that have taken place and still convert prices into the currency of their day. Conversations with supermarket staff along the lines of 'A piece of pumpkin that size used to be fourpence' only agitate the gum-chewing ones, causing them to roll up their eyes and ejaculate 'EH?' or, if they are feeling expansive, 'Yeah, yeah, Granddad.'

EXPERIENCE Acquired knowledge. Very common in the elderly, although frequently undervalued and underused by the general population, who generally appreciate its significance only when it is too late. Wisdom that comes with age is unwanted by the young, who would rather learn the hard way, as did the elderly in their time.

EXTRAVAGANT Wasteful. During the great Depression, extravagant meant having more than one piece of bread and dripping for the main meal. Today's superannuitants regard having more than one cream doughnut each week as extreme extravagance. See ECONOMY.

FACE The mirror of our emotions. The face is the most pampered part of the body — powdered, creamed, shaved, massaged, toned and even, occasionally, rearranged by surgeons. Some believe the face shows life's experiences; if this theory was correct, it would mean that most owners had spent their lives in the hill country of the South Island. Myriad preparations are available to reduce WRINKLEs, but these need to be applied frequently. There is also the risk of ending up with a face that appears not to belong to one's body. For example, a woman of my acquaintance who is now aged seventy-two still has her dimples and skin which is often likened to a particularly smooth portion of a baby's anatomy, having used fourteen tonnes of anti-wrinkle preparation during her lifetime (at a cost too frightening to calculate). Unfortunately the rest of her skin more closely resembles crushed velvet.

FAMILY Close relatives, often supportive and regarded with great affection by the elderly. The meaning of this term has altered considerably in recent times, and it has become rather unfashionable. It is often used in tandem with 'broken', 'single-parent', 'at-risk' and fragmented'.

Fashion

The elderly still prefer to use the term in its original sense, unless they are called upon to house members of their own family for longer than three days, when it tends to take on less positive overtones.

FARM A productive portion of land. In earlier times farm work provided employment for large numbers of people, but more recently the need for farm workers has decreased as a result of the introduction of computers, advisers and modern methods of farming. Many farmers now wear three-piece suits and work from executive chairs in front of computer monitors.

Future farmers will be trained laboratory technicians, and their farms will house one prime lamb and a thousand test tubes, containing cloned cells from the prime lamb donor. The new technology will not reduce the price of loin chops, however.

FARTHING A coin of minute value, which was nevertheless included in the price of many items. A favoured price was elevenpence three farthing. Beloved of drapers and confectioners, the farthing caused frustration and incipient insanity among their staff before the introduction of the electronic cash register and the desk calculator, by which time it was redundant anyway.

FASHION The clothing of the day. Fashion formerly included frocks, dresses, skirts, trousers, shirts and cardigans, but today it is made up of items such as T-shirts, sportswear, wrinkle-free suits, drip-dry shirts, leggings, bikinis and combat pants. Fashion is almost totally ignored

Fat

by the elderly, who are still wearing the frocks, cardigans and occasionally walkshorts of yesteryear. See TASTE.

FAT A bodily deposit resulting from certain dietary habits, and often associated with lack of EXERCISE. The word fat is now commonly used in a derogatory sense. There are few products sold specifically for the purpose of creating additional fat (although many which incidentally have that effect) but there are many, possibly thousands, sold for the purpose of reducing fat. These usually come complete with very expensive programmes and advisers, many of whom are overweight because of the diet they enjoy in their own homes, having successfully created feelings of guilt and loss of self-worth in their clients.

FELINE A term applied to the cat family. Many felines are kept as domestic pets, but this does not usually include the larger members of the family such as lions, because of the size of the modern home. Cats are the most pampered of animals, often having their own beds, rooms, toilets, food containers and fluffy rugs, all of which some elderly people would give their remaining teeth to enjoy. Cats are often fastidious animals, and their owners can spend many hours attempting to discover the correct diet for their pet, and even longer cleaning the carpet of its stomach contents after the chosen diet has been found to be unacceptable.

FERTILE Another word never used to describe the elderly.

Flagon

FIDELITY The state of being faithful. Not considered to be important in the modern world, where the young demand constant change. Couples who manage to remain married for fifty years or more tend to have their fidelity publicised in the newspapers. Judging by present trends it is likely that in the future this will occur after a period of ten years, and will gradually diminish even more, eventually covering the duration of the honeymoon (although not its cost).

FILM Formerly known as a 'picture'. 'Going to the pictures' used to be the entertainment highlight of the week. The plot always ensured that the hero eventually won the heroine, and the 'picture' often contained scenes of dancing, singing and comedy. The bad people wore dark clothes and were always caught and punished. Perhaps more unbelievable to today's young is that all of the actors managed to keep their clothes on throughout the entire film.

FISH An animal that has gills and scales; a sea dweller. Once commonly eaten, now scarce and, if available, very expensive. Often regarded as a 'brain food', its scarcity and price may account for the peculiar behaviour of many young.

FLAGON A once essential container which has been replaced in modern times by the much smaller can. Frequent users often stored empty flagons in their garages, some having to leave their cars outside when the number of flagons grew too large. Flagon collections

Flatulence

were regarded as assets, the owner eventually cashing in 'the empties' and replacing them with full ones at the local hotel following a series of losses at the races.

FLATULENCE A subject not referred to in company, but which exists despite efforts to conceal it. Flatulent people tend to gurgle, emitting a noise similar to the boiling mud of Rotorua. The only way to obtain relief is to remove oneself from company and find an uninhabited part of the property, preferably outside, where the build-up of gas can be released.

FOREFATHERS People from whom we are descended; those who determined our genetic inheritance and can be blamed for most personality and bodily defects. This is very useful, as we never have to admit responsibility for our appearance or temperament.

FOREFATHERS

Funeral

FORTUNE A mythical term describing the accumulation of wealth. Most elderly people are still seeking their fortune, but have possibly left the search too late, being too busy working to have made any headway. Related to the fable regarding the pot of gold and the rainbow.

FRACTURE A break. The most common fractures are concerned with the most expensive china. These cannot be remedied. The results of such fractures can be seen in boxes in auction rooms, where 'sets'of crockery can be made up of four cups, three saucers and one dinner plate. Other fractures are more serious and involve bones. Little sympathy is given to sufferers of bone fractures, who are told to 'be more careful in future' by clinical staff, and subjected to sighs of long-suffering on the part of their close relatives.

FRAME An apparatus used to aid walking, sometimes known as a walker. It consists of bent pipes and wheels, the bends in the frame often being the result of ramming the apparatus into the bodies of those who are impeding the progress of the user. Frequently seen being used by those with a FRACTURE.

FRIGID A term frequently used in association with the elderly.

FUNERAL A type of party in which the principal figure (the 'deceased') takes little or no part. Their essential role is to make sure they have saved enough to cover its cost before it occurs. Funerals are generally attended by

Furniture

friends and family, as well as varying numbers of hangers-on who have had little or nothing to do with the deceased, but enjoy a large, free afternoon tea, followed by drinks, and the opportunity to reminisce at length (see BOREDOM). Among family members funerals are often a time to release emotion and let others know what you really think of them. See also EULOGY.

FURNITURE The larger pieces of equipment occupying a home. Some furniture usually survives into old age, despite the attempts of one's children to reduce it to matchwood, one's cat using it for claw sharpening, one's dog for chewing, and the appearance of rings caused by wet glasses, spills, hot plates, etc. The earlier invention of Formica would have alleviated the need for furious polishing, prolonging the life of the owner as well as the furniture.

GARBAGE Formerly called rubbish, which used to be placed in steel containers called rubbish tins. These were placed at the gate for weekly collection by slow-moving vehicles staffed by polite operators. Today's rubbish consists mainly of plastic, tins, cardboard and unsolicited mail, all of which need to be separated and placed in individual containers. The volume of rubbish has increased fourfold, thus making it necessary to make four trips down the drive on rainy mornings, rather than the single weekly stagger of previous years.

GARLIC In earlier times invariably associated with 'foreigners', garlic is now frequently used in New Zealand kitchens. Its pungent odour can be detected on exhaled breath in many places, including clubs, restaurants and homes, and even among the members of HANDICRAFT groups. Garlic is claimed by some to have beneficial medicinal properties, and when taken in this way it means the claimant is living alone, in a pest- and vampire-free home.

GAY Once used to describe the feeling of being happy and lighthearted, the meaning of this term has altered considerably in recent years. Using this word in most rugby clubs will result in rapid ejection, although there are now even one or two 'gay' rugby teams, fortunately confined to large cities.

In establishments where testosterone levels are lower than in the traditional rugby club, use of the word 'gay' may draw other males to the user, with offers of Harvey Wallbangers and other exotic drinks. Caution is advised in all cases.

GEEZER An older person, usually male. Generally used in a derogatory sense when the subject has caused annoyance to a belligerent person by passing the time of day with them. Also incorrectly used to describe a plume of hot steam and water that erupts out of the ground at regular intervals.

GENERATION A new generation occurs when the children replace the parents as leaders in the family and community, making the parents the previous generation. This used to take place when the parents were in their seventies, but may now occur when children are as young as seven years old, when they take over the running of the household and hold its members to ransom. Attempts by parents to control this behaviour and remain the dominant generation may result in retaliation from social agencies, who will uphold the rights of the children at all costs.

GENIAL Happy and friendly; elderly people who are genial are often regarded with suspicion (see CRANK).

Gentlewoman

The state of being happy is a dying art and those fortunate enough to experience the condition are often thought of as having a drink problem, or smoking a type of pseudo-tobacco that smells like a garden bonfire.

GENIUS Having great intellect. All elderly are geniuses in their chosen fields; for example: 'Your aunt is the best pikelet maker — a pikelet genius,' 'The lady in the next flat knits woollen hats and scarves — she's a knitting genius.' Perhaps the most useful genius is the one who has mastered the art of home brewing, so that the product almost tastes like real beer.

GENTLEMAN A male who is aware of the correct way to behave in any situation; one of the better-known definitions of a gentleman is someone who always says pardon before removing his boots. Today gentlemen are almost extinct, like the moa, but not for the same reason.

GENTLEWOMAN All women are gentle, as any of them will tell you. Gentlewomen have an iron will and fierce determination, which are essential to maintain gentility while caring for a husband, children and a house. Many men, particularly gentlemen, are not aware of these qualities in their wives, as they are often carefully concealed beneath a polished veneer of docility and good manners.

In the less active sense, a gentlewoman may be defined as someone who places paper doilies under cakes when serving afternoon tea to her guests.

Girdle

GIRDLE A type of scone, the recipe for which originated in Scotland. Also a type of garment, no longer fashionable, which has been replaced by a newer innovation called dieting. Some people believe that girdles were invented because of heavy scone consumption, thus linking the two, although there is no scientific proof that this is the case.

GIRTH The measurement around an object. Used in clothing stores by assistants who measure elderly people with special tape measures that give higher readings. This causes great distress in the elderly, who falsely believe their girth is increasing, despite restricting their consumption of GIRDLE scones.

GLAMOROUS Another word that is never associated with the elderly, except when they are recalling their long-distant youth. This usage invariably induces stifled guffaws in younger members of the family.

GOLDEN Found in the phrase 'golden years', a term used to describe retirement or later life. It is believed to have originated in America, where large numbers of gold-capped teeth are displayed by the elderly.

GOOD OLD DAYS A term used by the elderly to describe their youth, regardless of the fact that they may have endured war, the Depression and poverty. The corollary is to be found in the oft-repeated sentence: 'You young blokes today don't know you're alive' (which, incidentally, is a very effective way of emptying the room).

Gramophone

GORGEOUS Rarely associated with the elderly, but used by them when describing pavlova and, occasionally, grandchildren.

GOUT A misunderstood disease which causes great mirth among non-sufferers, who persist in associating it with the consumption of excessive quantities of port. It usually attacks the big toe, which swells painfully and adopts vivid red and purple hues. Succinctly described by an anonymous New Zealand poet in the line 'You cannot get about, when you have a bout of gout.'

GRAMOPHONE A wonderful invention which played music and other forms of entertainment stored on records. Gramophones required winding and needles,

GRAMOPHONE

Grey

which added to their mystique. Transportable types of gramophone were often used to create a romantic ambience in unlikely areas, and were responsible for many engagements. Rarely seen today, having been replaced by technology such as stereos, Walkmans and 'ghettoblasters', which have no association with romance and are more likely to be used for anti-social purposes. Gramophones are, however, sometimes heard in Napier during 'Art Deco' weekends.

GREY A colour associated with the elderly – in particular their hair. Grey Power is an association formed to promote the political aspirations of the elderly, which also serves as a social and educational organisation. Many members of Grey Power are known to have voted for the politicians they now despise, thus bringing into question the cliché 'You are never too old to learn.' Members also play bingo.

GROCER Previously a person who sold groceries, generally to be found behind a shop counter. Grocers greeted their customers by name, and moved around the shop to obtain their requirements, which were then promptly and courteously delivered. (See GOOD OLD DAYS.) Today's grocers are members of the boards of large companies situated in the main centres, who have never handled a packet of flour and have no interest at all in knowing the names of their customers.

GRUMBLE A term used to describe comments made by the elderly when they complain of being served cold

Gymnasium

tea in coffee shops, or comment on the difference between service in the supermarket of today and by the GROCER of the past.

GYMNASIUM A Greek word, now used to describe an establishment where members can go to 'work out' by lifting weights, jumping, stretching, leaping and generally overexerting themselves to the point of exhaustion. Most elderly are sensible enough to avoid these establishments, partly through an inability to imagine how they could possibly get into, or out of, the required dress.

HABIT
1. The dress worn by members of religious orders. In the past this clothing made them instantly recognisable, especially to their former pupils, who were thus able to modify their language and general demeanour when the habit-wearer came into sight. Today's habits are much less distinctive and allow their wearers to blend into the community, much to the embarrassment of their past pupils.
2. Certain regular or set forms of behaviour. Habits may be good (such as washing the dishes prior to retiring for the night) or bad (such as leaving one's teeth out when the grandchildren come to visit). Many elderly people belatedly realise that 'good' habits are often in fact unimportant and not worth observing, a fact that today's young seem to be aware of from birth.

HACKLE As in 'getting the hackles up', and applied to elderly people who become aggressive when displeased. The unwary should endeavour to recognise the early signs of hackles rising, thus avoiding physical damage from walking sticks and other items of geriatric hardware.

Handicraft

HAGGIS A type of meat pudding, eaten on special occasions by those of Scottish persuasion. Probably invented by Robert Burns (a Scottish songwriter), haggis is eaten on Burns Night, which commemorates the birth of this famous man. On such occasions the haggis assumes human status, being 'piped in' by a Scottish person wearing a kilt and playing the bagpipes; this status is not surprising, since the haggis includes some of the essential organs associated with humans and higher animals, such as lungs, stomachs, livers and hearts. The main purpose of the haggis is believed to be to provide an excuse to consume large quantities of Scotch whisky, without which it is absolutely inedible.

HAIR A thin, string-like substance which once grew on the head. Hair required cutting at frequent intervals, an operation which used to be carried out in barbershops by loquacious experts who were aware of the form and prospects of every racehorse in the country. Today these experts have been replaced by young ladies in salons, who have no interest in horses (or old men), and only speak occasionally to ask if you have 'anything on tonight', a ridiculous question to which 'Baywatch' seems an inadequate reply. Some elderly men still have full heads of hair, but these are regarded with suspicion by the majority, who label them lotharios.

HANDICRAFT The manufacture of objects by hand, most of which are of no practical use, and some of which are unfathomable. Some people make wooden toys, while others who are more artistic paint land-

Harum-scarum

scapes, dress dolls, manufacture cards and create a variety of gifts, which they disperse liberally among their friends at Christmas time. Unfortunately their friends generally feel constrained to praise their efforts, so perpetuating this regrettable habit. See also CROCHET.

HARUM-SCARUM Now rarely heard, this expression was used to describe those who were reckless enough to perfom such acts as riding a bicycle at night without lights, passing the local policeman in the process, and other similar behaviour.

HAT A garment used as a head covering, which varies in shape and style according to the fashion of the day. In the past gentlemen wore top hats, bowlers, trilbies and shooting hats, while those of Scottish persuasion preferred glengarries and tam-o-shanters, which are still

HANDICRAFT

to be seen during the curling season in the South Island. Ladies' hats varied much more than men's, some resembling the interior of a church during harvest festival, while others were very plain, consisting of single wisps or strips of material; incomprehensibly, these were invariably the most expensive. Each hat was unique (to be seen in the same hat as another woman was a matter of considerable shame), and hats were designed to be so ridiculous as to make a woman's whereabouts obvious to her husband from a distance, so that he could successfully avoid being seen in her company.

Today, ladies reserve their best creations for major race meetings, where they once again compete for the prize of most ludicrous design. Male headgear now consists of caps, usually worn with the peak facing backwards, bearing slogans such as Those Damned Seagulls, Captain, Ford, Chicago Bulls, Hello Sailor and Carters Supplies.

HEADACHE A pain in the head. A useful affliction when one wants to avoid a stressful situation, such as a family gathering or neighbourhood-watch meeting. On these occasions even paracetamol will not offer any relief, and the only solution is to retire to a quiet room, preferably with a large Scotch and a television set showing the cricket.

HEARSE A vehicle for carrying those who were not fortunate enough to reach the top of a hospital waiting list (see HEART), thus saving the government the cost of an operation which would have prolonged their life. The

Heart

hearse is usually a splendidly appointed vehicle, and one which few people could afford to hire and ride in while still living.

HEART A very important organ. Heart surgery has made impressive strides in recent years, with the result that elderly people requiring urgent surgery are now placed on a waiting list, prior to being placed on another waiting list, before joining those on the short list, a misnomer as this list usually contains at least four hundred names. In recent years the government has halved waiting lists very effectively by simply removing hundreds of names from them, thus proving to the world that the numbers of sick are decreasing in New Zealand. This is in fact true, as large numbers of people die before they reach the top of the waiting list, thus improving the ratio of healthy to sick people.

HEAVEN A place in the sky where the spirits of the departed reside (see FUNERAL, HEARSE). An unsubstantiated rumour has it that even some politicians, lawyers, car salesmen and doorknockers of various religious persuasions dwell there, making the alternative to heaven, known as hell, increasingly appealing.

HEIR The person who inherits the fruits of one's lifetime labours, known as an inheritance. This is eagerly anticipated by many, but frequently squandered when they finally receive it. Small inheritances may consist only of the FLAGON collection housed in the shed, while others can be as large as half the South Island.

Hip

HENNA A plant dye. Perhaps the first-ever product used by women to alter the colour of their hair. The bright red colour produced caused the user to be ostracised by the female members of church congregations and other groups, who considered her to be fast, dizzy and – perhaps the more crushing term – a HUSSY. Men were much more tolerant, generally at least taking the trouble to try and find out whether they really deserved these labels.

HEYDAY The time when you thought you were at the height of your physical strength and attractiveness. A similar term is 'in one's prime', which some elderly people still like to think they are. Those with full-length mirrors are rapidly disabused of this idea, however.

HIP A major joint, which plays a vital part in swinging the legs to assist with walking, cycling, vacuum cleaning and a wide range of other activities. The hip joint often becomes painful, and movement impaired, as the result of the onset of ARTHRITIS. When the condition becomes unbearable, surgery is required, but it is seldom performed as it is cheaper to supply the sufferer with copious quantities of aspirin and letters written by faceless hospital staff who will never suffer from this condition because they are constantly seated in air-conditioned offices.

For a brief period hip also meant something akin to DEBONAIR, something an ARTHRITIS sufferer rarely feels.

Hose

HOSE A general term for stockings and socks, or leg coverings, which were formerly made of rayon or wool. Various methods were used to hold hose in place, including suspenders, garters, pieces of string (in lower socio-economic groups) and rubber bands, all of which were reputed to cause the wearer to suffer varicose veins in later life.

'Stockings' became a highly emotional issue when they were linked to the American armed services, who used the scarce nylon stocking as a form of currency. 'Nylons' were bartered for goods and favours bestowed by the ladies during the Second World War, and wearing nylons at that time was a sure indication that a lady had made a visiting American very welcome in this country. Some modern types of stockings are aptly called tights; these do away with the need for suspenders, and have absolutely no romantic appeal.

HOSPITAL An establishment which used to be for the treatment of the sick. Now used mainly as offices for administrators, who control vastly diminished numbers of doctors and nurses, with a sprinkling of patients. For a time hospitals were known as CHEs, perhaps in the hope that since no-one knew what the term meant they might stop going to them. Elderly people requiring surgery should consider visiting the 'Do-It-Yourself' section of their local public library. See also HEARSE, HEART.

HOUSE A dwelling that was formerly considered an essential aspiration, for which you made sacrifices and paid large sums of money, considerably in excess of its true value, due to interesting legal papers called mortgages. Lawyers and real estate agents find houses to be a constant source of revenue, which they use to buy expensive cars. Older people tend to live in flats, which are similar to houses but have more power points.

HUSSY Formerly a woman who used to dye her hair. See HENNA, HOSE.

I

IF A word that is frequently used by the elderly, often in the phrase 'If only'. Sentences which begin 'If only' usually signal accounts of what are considered to have been missed opportunities, and are generally a warning to visiting members of the family that it is time to go home. See BOREDOM.

ILL The state of being unwell. Most conditions causing one to be unwell are now treated with chemical preparations, the side effects of which are far worse than the original illness.

IMAGINE Similar to IF, but requiring the ability to use the mind to envisage happenings which have never happened and never will. See AMAZING.

IMMACULATE A term which describes the short-lived appearance of the elderly when they have just dressed for the day, and before they have consumed food or drink.

IMMIGRATION When a person leaves a less desirable environment for a better life in a new country. This applies to many of New Zealand's elderly people, who

Improvise

left the unbreathable air of 'Home' for the fresh air, good food and trout fishing of their newly adopted land.

IMMORAL A term not generally used to describe elderly activities. Formerly used to describe situations such as mixed-sex hand-holding, today it is more often used in conjunction with matters such as tax, big business and the government.

IMPERIAL To do with empires; once used as a title for royalty. Those of British origin will recall the observance of Empire Day, which was a day of endless BOREDOM. Today, used as a term for those in power in obscure African states, money for which is provided by benevolent governments such as New Zealand's, despite the length of our waiting lists (see HEART, HOSPITAL).

IMPOTENT A term frequently used to describe a condition of the elderly.

IMPREGNATE Never used to describe the results of any activity performed by the elderly, except in newspaper reports of septuagenarians who father large families in obscure and probably non-existent countries.

IMPROVISE The art of using what is available; being inventive. New Zealanders pride themselves on the ability to improvise (see NUMBER EIGHT WIRE), although there is evidence that this skill is diminishing in today's society. Notable improvisations include underwear made from flour sacks and soup made from salt and

Incapable

IMPROVISE

water, both common during the great Depression. The underwear users formed a highly successful team known as the Champion High Grade.

INCAPABLE Younger members of the family often view their elderly relatives as incapable. In fact, any person who has lived longer than sixty years is quite obviously capable.

INCISORS The front teeth. Always the first to be extracted or to drop out. This leaves their bereft owner with a vastly changed appearance and with limited ability to successfully masticate any food other than soft sausage, mashed potato and custards. Kissing the grandchildren, however, provides them with a totally new experience.

In-growing

INCREMENT An increase. Pension increments are linked to the rate of inflation, and also linked to the basic wage. A better scheme would be to link them to the parliamentary wage, which would instantly make superannuitants millionaires.

INDIGESTION The inability of the body to process food which has been consumed, causing feelings of discomfort and sometimes pain. Indigestion used to be experienced frequently following a Monday lunch of very dry sandwiches, a consequence of the lack of fresh bread on Sundays. The condition is often experienced by the elderly, who are frequent patrons of fast food outlets.

INEBRIATION A state of incoordination caused by the onset of an emotional upset or a communicable disease. Sometimes incorrectly attributed to consuming too much alcohol.

INFLUENZA An infectious disease to which the elderly have absolute immunity, as a result of free vaccinations offered by general practitioners. Most take up this offer, unable to resist the opportunity to get something for nothing.

IN-GROWING Generally used in association with toenails. A painful complaint which commits the sufferer to going without footwear until the offending nail is removed. Also used in an uncharitable way to describe baldness, referred to as in-growing hair.

Intercourse

INTERCOURSE Social communication. Common among the elderly, not to be confused with sexual intercourse; the elderly also engage in this form of communication, but rarely admit to this, particularly to younger members of their family, who generally react with disbelief and disgust.

INVIGORATE To swallow a mixture of pills to achieve youthful energy. Similar to having access to the fountain of youth, at least according to the pill-makers, but in more convenient compressed-powder form.

IRISH Many immigrants to New Zealand are from the Emerald Isle. They are excellent workers, especially within the building and construction field. Their most noticeable contribution to New Zealand is marked by the naming of hotels such as The Rose and Shamrock, and serving of green beer and green sausages on St Patrick's Day. One person of Irish descent has risen to the office of Prime Minister of New Zealand, but was later deposed by a woman of non-Irish descent (contrary to popular belief this act was not the origin of the term 'gone for a Burton').

IRON An element essential to the maintenance of good health. Many elderly were fed large, steaming bowls of silver beet when they were young, and some even continue to consume this substance today. A few footballers and extremely wealthy modern families acquire iron by eating large steaks, but the majority prefer to take their iron in the form of a pill.

Ivy

IRRESISTIBLE Another word never used to describe the elderly.

IRRITABLE Often used to describe the elderly, and a condition that they often induce in their families; being annoyed. Almost all things in the modern world could be listed as causes of irritation in the elderly, notable exceptions being 'Coronation Street', 'The Young and the Restless' and, among males, the delayed screening of Super Twelve rugby (few elderly people can afford Sky).

IVY A grand old name. Also a creeping plant which gradually envelops objects; most men would like to meet a girl named Ivy who has the attributes of the plant, but few ever do.

J

JAM

JACK OF ALL TRADES This title can be applied to many elderly people, who, through a resourceful attitude combined with lack of funds to pay tradesmen, have developed skills in a range of areas. Many of these skills are employed to repair items belonging to grandchildren, who either do not understand the concept of 'repairing', or believe it means getting in the car and driving to a 'repair shop'.

Job

JAM Jam-making is an art passed down from generation to generation, at least until the present. Today the art shows signs of dying out, as the young do not consider jam-making an essential skill but a laughable occupation their mothers and grandmothers undertook to fill their empty days. Most 'jam' today is bought from supermarkets; this substance bears little relation to the original, however, being a by-product from glue factories.

JAZZ The mad, rapid beat music which was danced to in the thirties. Still in vogue today among a few discerning persons who retain the ability to enjoy themselves.

JERSEY A type of bovine animal. Also an indispensable article of clothing. In the past females used to knit jerseys for males as a sign of affection. Men were powerless to prevent this activity, which inspired dread among most of them, as it generally signalled the female's desire for an early engagement. In addition, the end product was often an object that caused deep embarrassment to the recipient, as it frequently came in highly imaginative colours, usually had one sleeve at least six inches longer than the other, and was either three sizes too big or one size too small (which was possibly because it would have been considered unseemly for the female to come close enough to the male to take his measurements).

JOB Work for which one was paid. Now disappearing as a means of earning enough money to provide for one's family, jobs have largely been replaced by 'welfare'. Contrary to the belief widely held by the wealthy, 'wel-

Jug

fare' is not the choice of those who are unemployed, but the result of businesses 'restructuring', a recent term that means increasing profits without considering people. In an unusually strong consensus, most of the population are hoping that Parliament will be considered for restructuring, removing at least two-thirds of its members, which would save vast amounts of money and reduce public frustration to a manageable level. There is some opposition to this move from Wellington taxi-drivers, however, who would face a huge drop in business.

JUG A receptacle for holding liquids. The milk jug (now almost completely obsolete) was a significant household item which was always produced at meal times, being draped with a handmade cover (see CROCHET, HANDICRAFT) often festooned with beads. This was an effective method of keeping blowflies out of the liquid.

Beer jugs used to be made of glass, but these have now been replaced with the plastic variety, which cause less damage when used as projectiles.

'Hey, Jugs,' is a term of affection directed at people with large EARS, while being 'in the jug' is a euphemism roughly comparable with a female's 'going up north for a while' i.e. out of circulation until a temporary problem blows over.

JUMBLE Disorder. Now replaced by the word wardrobe. Many elderly people rely on 'jumble sales' for their clothing requirements, hence the periodic resurgence of Crimplene suits with flared trousers. One could be forgiven for thinking that many fashionable (not to be confused with GLAMOROUS) young people also acquire their clothing in the same way.

JUVENILE Youthful. The behaviour resorted to by the elderly at Christmas time. This often results in elderly men being slapped by young ladies when they carry their juvenile fantasies too far.

KAOLIN A medical preparation used frequently as a poultice. Kaolin is spread on a cloth and heated in the oven at 200° C for twenty minutes, then immediately applied to the skin, where it produces third-degree burns. The patient rarely has the courage to complain of further symptoms, so the kaolin is regarded by the medical profession as providing a miraculous cure.

KEROSENE A fossil fuel having many uses, claimed to include freeing seized bearings, cleaning charred frying pans, heating the house and washing down paint. Absolute believers take it as a medicinal preparation in very small quantities, while as a bath cleaner it was used to scour the bath and also impart a sheen on the surfaces of both bath and bather; the smell is said to wear off the skin of the bather within 24 hours (see CRANK).

KETTLE An obsolete item (today replaced by the electric jug) which used to be the most important thing in the kitchen, closely followed by the dripping tin, without which cooking was restricted to boiling. The kettle always contained hot water, providing a constant

Kiss

supply of tea throughout the day, and the handle was highly polished as a result of its frequent use.

KIPPER A type of smoked herring, and a popular breakfast dish among those of British origin. Kipper-eating was a difficult artform to master, with few consumers ever attaining great proficiency. The kipper contained several million fine bones, and took at least an hour to eat, so it was only ever popular with early risers, who could enjoy it and still manage to get to work on time. The kipper has never caught on as a culinary experience in this country.

KISS A pleasant contact, a lip caress. Kisses are common during courtship, but decrease in frequency in direct proportion to the number of years of marriage. Passionate kissing is strictly forbidden among the elderly,

KIPPER

Knacker

and public displays of this nature are regarded as obscene. Most elderly rely on their grandchildren for bestowing and receiving kisses, although those with beards should be cautious, as the young can react unpredictably when they come into close contact with facial hair.

KNACKER A person who disposes of old horses and cattle. The term 'knackered' is often used by elderly men in reply to the question 'How are you?' This is particularly common the day after a visit by one's family, but may apply after a hard day's bowling or an evening sitting up in front of 'Baywatch'.

KNEE The largest joint in the body, possibly because of arthritic swelling, which makes it enlarge to gigantic proportions. Now replaceable by surgeons, but mostly in private hospitals. Knees used to be favourite sitting spots of grandchildren, but today this activity is regarded as dangerous and not to be encouraged.

LACE A string, often woven, which is used to keep footwear in place. Once comfortably within the reach of the owner, but less accessible and requiring greater effort to tie as age increases. Lace is also used as a decoration on some women's clothing, improving its appearance and making the wearer even more appealing to males. Some lace garments are never seen by any male who considers himself a GENTLEMAN, even on washdays.

LACE

Lad

LAD A young male. 'When I was a lad' is a phrase often used by elderly men, to the great disgust of the young. See also GOOD OLD DAYS.

LADY A female who is well-mannered and cultured, genteel, kind, softly spoken, welcoming, loving, serene, polite and well-groomed. Also known as a wife. Not a HUSSY.

LADY-KILLER Originally a murderer, one who had caused the demise of a lady, a grave offence punishable by hanging.

Now used to describe an even more despicable person, one who trifles with the gentle sex by adopting false manners and dress, with the aim of inveigling their way into a lady's affections. Such persons are often seen at singles dances and in clubs on Saturday evenings. Caution is advised.

LAMB A young animal of the sheep family. Once cheap and plentiful, and an important part of the New Zealand diet. Now considered a luxury, lamb chops only being served on special occasions such as end-of-year bowling-club barbecues.

LARD The rendered fat of the pig. Once an indispensable commodity in the kitchen, now frowned upon by those who are concerned with cholesterol levels (another American discovery which has completely altered our eating habits). Lard has largely been replaced with lettuce, although not in pastry making.

Liniment

LASSIE A term used by those of Scottish persuasion to refer to a young lady.

LAVENDER A fragrant shrub, the flowers of which are used in a variety of ways by the ladies. Lavender is an ingredient of perfumes and cosmetics, and is also placed among clothing to impart a pleasing fragrance and deter moths. In the past lavender was used as an aftershave and male perfume, such preparations being known as toilet water. Males using these preparations were often regarded with suspicion by other males, whose preferred perfume was a splash of bay rum, following a one-and-sixpenny haircut, prior to the Saturday dance.

LEISURE Used to mean spare time. Having excess leisure time is called retirement. Most leisure time during retirement is directed to the maintenance and repair of houses and equipment belonging to one's immediate family. For those with large families these activities take up most of the daylight hours, leaving only Sunday afternoons for the pursuit of much needed rest.

LESS A word which is commonly applied to the purchasing power of the dollar. The elderly also use it in association with teeth, hair, money and power, but rarely in association with weight.

LINIMENT A medicinal preparation containing volatile oils, which is rubbed into bruised or strained body parts. Some elderly men who have never recovered from not

Liquorice

being selected for the All Blacks use liniment as a body lotion. This tends to earn them the ridicule of their friends, and indeed anyone in the immediate vicinity.

LIQUORICE A medicinal substance produced from a plant root. In the past it was often mixed with other unmentionable medicaments into a paste, and administered to the young on Friday nights. Similar dosing may have included sulphur and molasses, Epsom salts, Lane's Emulsion and cod liver oil.

LOAN To lend. In connection with one's family the term loan is more accurately replaced with 'give'; most elderly have long since learnt not to expect the return of money or goods 'loaned' to close family members.

LODGER A person who resides in another's home as a paying guest. Today this term has been largely replaced by the word flatmate. Lodging was very common in New Zealand in the past, and lodgers were often accommodated in boarding houses which had strict rules enforced by formidable lady owners. Few paying guests were foolish enough to argue with the proprietor of their boarding house, as this could invoke penalties such as being given lumpy porridge for a week (for minor disagreements) or (for more serious matters) ejection on to the street with no consideration of the weather.

Male lodgers were often unjustly accused of ungentlemanly behaviour with their landlady's attractive daughters. A more serious accusation was of 'carrying on' with the proprietor herself in the absence of her husband.

Luxury

Despite the widely held view that husbands are stupid, unobservant and insensitive, they would invariably sense this behaviour when the lady of the house served the lodger first, or offered him the one remaining portion of pudding.

LOVE Fondness for or strong attraction to someone or something. Every elderly person has experienced this emotion, usually when in the company of their beloved. In later life the word takes on a different significance, being used to describe extreme fondness for oysters, rugby, cream sponges and various other edibles.

LUCK Good (or bad) fortune. To be lucky in LOVE means to have chosen a compatible lifelong partner. Other forms of luck include constantly winning the bowling club's weekly raffle or doing well at the races. Luck is notoriously fickle, and delights in letting one down just when one needs it most.

LUST A sin, particularly in the elderly, who are well-advised to conceal any lustful inclinations.

LUXURY Once meant having many belongings of above-average quality and habitually dining out on rare and expensive foods. As one becomes older one's definition of luxury changes, so that by the time one is elderly it means sitting in a comfortable chair in front of a blazing log fire, enjoying tea and gingernut biscuits.

M

MAJORITY Having a greater number than anyone else. When applied to governments, the term means receiving more votes than any other party. MMP is a form of government that allows a party to govern without necessarily having a majority.

MALAISE A feeling of illness, often experienced while watching the television news or a live broadcast of the New Zealand cricket team. The feeling is particularly common when Members of Parliament are quoted at length, or when rugby players break down and apologise tearfully for getting drunk after losing a game. (Cricket players do not seem to have this tendency, perhaps because they are more accustomed to losing.)

MALAPROPISM Using the wrong words, a common problem for the elderly, who find it difficult to keep up with changes in modern usage; see, for example, GAY. 'Cool' is another word often misused by the elderly; formerly meaning at a reduced temperature, it is now used to denote someone who is fashionable, desirable, perhaps even DEBONAIR. A 'cool' youth is someone who walks as if they have orthopedic problems and wear clothes that are five sizes too large for them. These are usually smothered in logos which are totally unintelligible to the elderly.

MALINGERER One who avoids work by feigning illness. Formerly used most often to describe someone who avoided going to school, the term is now applied to anyone who has had the misfortune to have an accident at work, thus making them eligible for ACC payments. 'Beneficiaries' are also frequently regarded as malingerers by politicians and people who live in Remuera or Fendalton.

MANAGE To use the available resources in the best possible ways. The elderly have always done this, and as a result have earned the labels 'mean', 'miserly' and 'parsimonious'. The phrase 'I can manage' is often heard coming from the elderly, usually in a highly irritated tone. (see FAMILY).

MANCHESTER A rainy city in the Midlands of England. Once famous for the manufacture of cotton and linen goods, prior to the invention of polyester/cotton and other mixed fabrics, which are convenient because they rarely require ironing (a dying art, never practised by the young), but entirely lack the sensual qualities of 'natural' fibres. This should not concern the elderly, who do not know the meaning of the word sensual, but it does — particularly elderly men, who never had to do the ironing.

Mangle

MANGLE A laundry appliance used to wring water from clothing. Many mangles were free-standing, with wooden rollers, while others were attached between two sinks, known as 'tubs'. Very hot washing was removed from the 'copper' on the end of a long stick and placed in the first tub, which was filled with water. It was then fed through the mangle, ending up in the second sink a lot lighter and not so hot. One of the dangers of mangles was that the biceps of one arm became more developed than those of the other, giving the mangle operator an asymmetrical appearance. The replacement of coppers and mangles by electric washing machines was a major factor in the EMANCIPATION of women.

MANNERS A semi-obsolete word, which previously meant socially acceptable behaviour. Manners are unknown to the young (see A/EH?), some of whom appear to communicate with a limited sign language, involving one, or sometimes two, fingers, particularly when they find themselves alongside elderly people at traffic lights.

MARGARINE Fake butter. Never used by the more discerning housewife, and totally ignored by dairy farmers and their families. Margarine was invented by the Americans to use up surplus grease and oils; many people did not realise at first that it was for eating, using it instead to ease squeaking hinges.

MARMALADE A type of jam made with citrus fruits.

Match

Marmalade is highly addictive, particularly among males of British extraction, for whom it is an essential part of the early-morning diet. These people often conceal themselves behind newspapers while eating it. Marmalade deprivation results in manic behaviour such as eye-rolling, arm-waving and hoarse shouting, which usually sends spouses out of the house to take refuge in the nearest supermarket.

The best marmalade is of course homemade, and makers and consumers enjoy endless discussion about the correct ingredients and their proportions (including the inclusion of items such as ginger and whisky) and the desired consistency.

MASTER A man of great authority. Some men erroneously believe they are the masters in their own homes, while their wives quietly go about their business knowing that the 'master' is totally dependent on them for his survival and wellbeing.

The term 'master' was previously bestowed on those of the teaching profession, but this practice has fallen into disuse with the altered status of teachers and pupils, and first names are preferred all round.

MATCH
1. A device for making fire. Most males used to carry matches in their pockets for lighting cigarettes and pipes, but with the decline in smoking matches are mainly used to light the barbecue in summer or the log fire in winter. In the past making a 'good match' was particularly important for women; this

had little to do with lighting fires, but referred to finding a suitable partner in life.
2. A game between two teams or individuals, e.g. a rugby or cricket match (in the latter case there is an increasing preference for the term 'mismatch').

MATRON The lady in charge of a hospital. Formerly matrons were formidable women who wore highly starched uniforms that crackled as they walked, and were much feared by staff and patients. Today these fearsome, but highly efficient, women have been replaced by people of both sexes who have imposing titles, resemble Business Studies graduates, and wear designer suits and expensive watches. They also carry pagers and cellphones, and some have been seen talking to and even smiling at patients.

MEAT The flesh of animals, in earlier times consumed in quantity. Now largely replaced by items such as pasta and multicoloured lettuce, particularly in restaurants.

MEDAL A metal object resembling a coin, awarded for service or achievement. Military medals are awarded to those who have spent a portion of their lives in the armed forces; this is cheaper for the government than providing for their present needs, such as hospital attention, and provides politicians with vital 'photo opportunities.

MEDICINE The art of healing. Also those substances used in the treatment of disease. The healing art is prac-

Melody

tised by highly trained professionals, and in many cases by the older members of the family, who use remedies handed down from generations past. Modern cures are attractively packaged, but not necessarily more effective than the home remedies that come out of tins and bottles in the kitchens of the knowledgeable. In the past the medical profession was regarded with respect and even fear; today doctors are a lot younger (often the age of one's older grandchildren) and encourage one to talk to them as equals, which can be just as frightening.

MELODY Sweet sounds; musical noises that are pleasant and tuneful. Melodies often trigger memories of enjoyable events in the past, although the music of today is more likely to trigger nightmares, it being difficult to

MEDAL

Memory

imagine any pleasant experience in relation to the cacophony made by The Blood Dripping Daggers, The Maniacal Vampire Choir or other similar orchestras popular today.

MEMORY The ability to recall the past. Memory may be acute, good, bad, or non-existent. Having an acute memory means that when you meet a friend after 45 years you still recall the five bob you lent them in 1953; good means you can remember what occurred more than five minutes ago; bad means you cannot recall beyond three minutes ago; while non-existent means ... Sorry! I've forgotten what I was about to write.

METRE A modern unit of measurement. The 'metric system' was adopted some years ago with the express purpose of confusing the elderly; it still causes great difficulty to many, who may be heard to say 'I'd like a kilometre of sausages, please,' 'I'll take thirteen kilograms of that material, please,' or, at the petrol pumps, 'Thirty millilitregrams, or twenty dollars' worth, whichever is greater.'

MILK A white fluid produced by cows. Milk once came in billies, JUGs, cans and bottles; it now comes in soft plastic 'sachets', which are impossible to open and usually result in the milk ending up on the floor, or in cardboard cartons, which can only be opened with difficulty; even the manufacturers admit this, and every so often try a new opening device, such as a funny plastic screw lid in the side of the cardboard carton.

Modern cows are well educated, and are now able to

Morals

produce milk that is fat-free, homogenised, calcium-enriched, farmhouse and full-cream.

MINCE A substance made by grinding up meat. Viewed with suspicion by the New Zealand housewife, because of the quality of the meat used and the fat content. Although the composition of mince has not changed over the years, it is now given attractive labels such as 'pure beef', 'topside', 'fat-lowered' and 'finest selected', which enables those who have to buy mince to pretend they are choosing it for its quality rather than its price.

MINT
1. An indispensable herb which is made into mint sauce and poured liberally over lamb or hogget. The art of making mint sauce is showing a tendency to die out, as it appears to be beyond the capabilities of the young, who believe all sauce comes from the supermarket in a bottle.
2. An establishment where money is made and stockpiled, e.g. the Inland Revenue Department.

MORALS Correct or approved behaviour. The meaning of this word has changed significantly over the years, and today it is almost obsolete. In the past a young lady's parents always attempted to assess the morals of a prospective suitor by inviting him to afternoon tea, at which time they would try to ascertain his true intentions regarding their daughter. A practised suitor would try to create a good impression by patting the family dog and stroking the cat, and being particularly attentive to the

Mother

young lady's mother. Of course, overdoing this could backfire, upsetting her father.

MOTHERS An underrated group of people, generally women, who bear children, raise children and husbands, and basically keep the country on the straight and narrow. Mothers are traditionally modest, unassuming, strong and unappreciated. In the defence of their families, however, they become fearsome and unbeatable, frequently reducing schoolteachers and other figures of 'authority' to tears.

MUTTON The meat of older sheep, full of flavour, which can be stewed, roasted, boiled or baked. In the past a staple part of the diet, mutton is now regarded less favourably and often classed as second grade. It is wonderful stewed with potatoes and onions to form a winter ambrosia called Irish stew; the smell of this cooking is even better than the aroma of a baking chocolate cake.

MYTH A tale that one does not expect to believe; for example, there are fairies at the bottom of the garden, and politicians always keep the promises they make prior to elections.

N

NAG A one-sided conversation that consists of fault-finding. Most men believe only women (particularly wives) nag, while all women know better. A horse may also be known as a nag; there is a connection, as wives have been known to nag if their husbands continually wager, and lose, the housekeeping money on a nag.

NAP A fundamental part of an elderly person's day. Naps, or short impromptu sleeps, are essential for good health and social equilibrium. Naps are often triggered by television programmes, and also by irrelevant conversation (see BORING). One should be careful about napping in company, which can have serious repercussions, and the napper should have a selection of excuses ready; for example, 'It's the new medication,' or 'I slept poorly last night.' Of course, it's hard to beat the classic excuse 'I wasn't asleep, I was just resting my eyes.' Too much public napping, or napping when one's spouse has something to say, can lead to NAGging.

NEWFANGLED Anything that is newer than 30 years old. The term is often used in connection with recently acquired items that the owner has trouble operating;

Nice

this particularly includes the newer varieties of telephone (usually bestowed on the elderly by thoughtful offspring who have no idea of the frustration they cause), radios (especially clock radios), cars, food mixers and vacuum cleaners. Some folk have never been able to master the operation of the zip fastener, and even class this in the newfangled category.

NICE Acceptable; the opposite of nasty. As a child, nice used to mean not pulling your cousins' hair, while nasty meant encouraging them to walk through the bull paddock. Nice people tend to end up as florists and those who sell HANDICRAFTS; nasty people tend to succeed in life, becoming managers and business tycoons. Generally,

NEWFANGLED

once people have succeeded past a certain point, others forget they are nasty and regard them as nice.

NIMBLE Being able to move swiftly, with AGILITY. See CRAMP.

NIP A pinch. An antisocial action which is not uncommon among present-day rugby players. A nip is also a measure of alcohol which forms the basis of a drink. An old-style nip meant you could actually taste the spirit of your choice when the soda or lemonade was added, in contrast to today's nips, of which several hundred are poured from a single bottle.

NONSENSE An illogical form of thought or speech. The word can also be used to describe parliamentary 'debate', and arguments about the rival 'qualities' of television newsreaders.

NOSY Having a large nose and being inquisitive. Many teenagers regard their parents as nosy, particularly when they want to know where they are going on a Saturday night, and with whom. Many elderly regard their offspring as nosy, particularly when they want to know how much is in their bank account, why they are still wearing those funny old slippers, and whether their bowels are working.

NUMBER EIGHT WIRE A useful material with which most New Zealand men believe they can make or fix anything. See MYTH.

Nutty

NUTTY Containing nuts, or having a nutty flavour. Essential in some confectionary, the enjoyment of which depends greatly on the state of one's teeth. The term has an unfortunate slang meaning, often used by the young to describe any group of elderly persons who are enjoying themselves. See also CRANK, ECCENTRIC.

NUZZLE To press or rub the nose against a person (not to be confused with the Maori term 'hongi'). Dog owners are very fond of nuzzling, while their visitors tend to react with distaste.

When one is betrothed, nuzzling plays an important part in the courtship; the nuzzler aims for the neck of the nuzzled, causing a giggling reaction, followed by a skin response commonly called 'goose pimples' (if I remember correctly).

OBSTETRIC Concerning the birth of babies. Once the sole domain of women, shrouded in secrecy, with the male playing absolutely no recognised part in the process. Today's fathers are encouraged, indeed expected, to attend the whole procedure, much to the unspoken horror of many.

ODD Not usual, or lacking one half of a pair. Odd socks are common among the elderly, as are odd thoughts. The odd cake or biscuit used to be required to be left on the plate at the conclusion of afternoon tea; the origin of this practice is obscure, but it is a tradition that is worth preserving, as it provides a chance for the exhausted host or hostess to enjoy a snack in peace after the guests have departed. See also CRANK.

OLD Once used to describe those who had attained the age of seventy, who were regarded with respect and even reverence. Today the term is used for people over the age of fifty, who are more commonly regarded as irrelevant, bothersome and a major source of embarrassment.

Olive

OLIVE A type of stone fruit previously only consumed by foreigners, mainly from the Mediterranean area. Until recently olives were seldom seen in New Zealand, other than in the better hotels, where they were placed in alcoholic drinks known as martinis. Today olive oil is used in many homes for cooking and in salad dressing, although this trend is unlikely ever to threaten the popular Highlander condensed-milk dressing.

OPPOSITION A type of political party whose purpose is to oppose government proposals, leading to 'debates' (see NONSENSE). Opposition parties often have great difficulty in finding proposals with which they disagree; the similarity between the various parties' proposals causes great confusion in the minds of voters, as well as in the minds of parliamentarians.

OPTOMETRIST A professional who detects eye defects and prescribes and supplies corrective lenses. In times past the eyes would be tested by the patient standing at a specified distance from a wall card and reading off the visible letters – a very simple procedure. Today technology has taken over, and the patient (aka the client) is seated in a space-age astronaut's chair and told to look into the astigmatic autorefrectometing analyser, while the airpressing glaucopuffer tester blows air on the eye. This equipment apparently costs millions of dollars, the cost being reflected in the consultation fee and the cost of lenses.

However, the examination and the bill, unnerving as they are, are nothing compared to choosing the frames

Orgy

for new spectacles. The patient is carefully steered into the frame department, where they are forced to make an instant choice from the hundreds of frames on display. Reaching for the frame of your choice will bring a slight, condescending smile to the delicate lips of the attractive assistant; 'That,' she will inform you, 'is the new Cappachio Spagetini Marsalario frame, designed in Italy.' When you force yourself to timidly enquire about the price, the charming assistant will name a figure which would have bought you a large block of land fifty years ago.

You then try to decide whether your next appointment should be with a mortgage broker or a psychologist.

OPULENT Having wealth. An uncommon condition of the elderly.

ORDER Laws and rules; having one's thoughts and belongings organised. Also used in the phrase 'Law and Order', matters, once maintained by police, who in recent times have been replaced by a computer, any call for assistance being answered by a floppy disk.

ORGY Once meant having two flagons of beer while listening to a Ranfurly Shield match on the radio. Now reputed to include various activities including debauchery (meaning unknown to the author) and licentious revelry (also unknown to the author). Orgies are believed to have originated in Ancient Rome, which probably accounts for the terrible condition of the once well-maintained Coliseum. Caution is advised.

Ornament

ORNAMENT An object used for adornment. In the home, ornaments often include unwanted wedding gifts, which are generally hidden away until the giver visits, when there is a sudden flurry of activity in order to identify the correct gift. The extremely orderly maintain lists of such gifts, together with the names of the givers.

OSTRICH A large African bird, once prized for its feathers. Today, fashionable people with overtly carnivorous appetites actually eat ostrich flesh.

OYSTER A bivalve mollusc. The best in the world are harvested at Bluff, New Zealand. This prized delicacy is treasured by connoisseurs, who eagerly await the commencement of the oyster season. Unfortunately, few people can actually afford to buy oysters, and only fanatics prepared to go without other food for a period of several weeks are able to indulge their passion.

OYSTER

PACE The speed at which one performs activities such as walking. Pace decreases with age, to the frustration of both young and old, and it would be interesting to know whether the incidence of road rage has increased proportionately with the number of elderly in the community.

The 'pacemaker' is a modern invention which controls the heart rate during normal activities, although it is not effective for more stressful situations such as filling in end-of-year tax returns.

PAINT A substance used to cover a surface, the colour varying according to taste. Once, all paint was beige; houses were not distinguished by their colour, making it difficult for revellers and winning gamblers to find their homes. Modern paints, which are designed to be used in particular settings, are very easy to apply but difficult to remove. Failure to obtain the desired result and subsequent complaints to the retailer lead to such replies as 'Your preparation was not correct,' or 'Oh dear! Who told you to use that? It's only for stainless steel bathrooms.'

'War paint' is not actually paint at all, but a cosmetic

concoction some women consider essential before they can leave the house. See also HUSSY.

PALM The inner part of the hand. Palmists 'read' one's hand to ascertain the future, and many clients apparently believe what they are told. Having consulted a palmist some fifty years ago, the author is still awaiting the birth of triplets and has not yet found the gold mine. There are always some people who can be 'palmed off' with a good story.

PANDEMONIUM A state that exists every morning in houses where there are three children and a husband.

PANTOMIME Parliament.

PAPER A news sheet. Much sought after by the elderly, who can fill a considerable portion of the day by studying its contents. Local papers detail all of the happenings in the community, ad nauseam, including accounts of local body meetings, court proceedings, weddings, births (not necessarily in that order), and the funerals of old identities. 'Metropolitan' papers also include overseas news such as the rise and fall of Burmese, Thai, Hong Kong and British currency, most of which few of us can understand or care about. Important occasions such as the start of the duck-shooting season also get full coverage, with a photograph showing the first limit bag shooter on the front page. Other significant events such as marriage breakdowns among rugby stars, pop singers and the royal family also feature regularly on the front page.

PARDON See FLATULENCE.

PARLIAMENT The governing body of the country. A group of people, some of whom have been elected, who hold the false belief that they are entrusted with the wellbeing and future of the citizens of the country (see MOTHER). These people are known collectively as 'parliamentarians'. In reality, they enjoy large salaries and perquisites, cheap food and drink, and the use of plush limousines and taxis. They often have strong acting abilities, but their debating skills rarely match those of a four-year-old child.

PARLOUR Previously the best room in the house, reserved for proposals, funerals, wedding breakfasts and christening parties, to which the rougher family elements were not invited; the room set aside to contain the most treasured family possessions.

Today a parlour is a place one goes to for massages or ice creams.

PARROT A bird that is capable of speaking words or phrases. Parrots make good companions for the elderly, often providing them with their most intelligent conversations of the day. Some caution is necessary, as parrots have a tendency to repeat bad language, especially in the presence of visitors.

PATIENT This word describes the demeanour of those who are awaiting admission to a healing institution. Once admitted, they are known as clients.

PEG Previously a wooden article used for securing clothing on washing lines; often handmade by skilled craftspeople. Bags and aprons for holding pegs were frequently sold at church fairs, etc. (see HANDICRAFTS). Today pegs are usually made of plastic, and come in a multitude of colours; this does not prevent the eternal problem of pegs disappearing, a phenomenon which has never been convincingly explained but does make them much less useful for making dolls and other traditional toys.

PENNY In times past a coin greatly treasured by the young; having a penny gave the owner great social standing within the primary-school community. The purchasing power of the penny was great, and included

PARROT

large bags of extremely sticky toffee (which would take hours to dissolve in the mouth), bags of biscuits or enormous ice-cream cones. Women were also known to 'spend a penny' on occasion, but this was not related to purchasing sweets.

PILE A heap. As in 'I have a pile of washing,' or 'He made his pile in real estate.' The medical use of the word refers to something quite different, which results from sitting on cold steps. Mothers frequently warn their young children to avoid this, causing confusion among children when they try to connect the medical condition with the wooden supports under the house. Many suffer from night terrors throughout childhood as a result.

PRETTY A term used to describe flowers, curtains and granddaughters. Rarely used to describe the elderly.

PUDDING A wonderful boiled food, which has largely fallen out of favour today. Puddings may be sweet, such as apple and treacle, or savoury, such as steak and kidney. All were delicious, although they frequently led to the need to take a NAP.

PUZZLE Aptly describes modern life.

QUADRUPLE To increase fourfold, generally applied to one's weight, taxes, the cost of food and mortgages. Seldom used with reference to one's bank balance or savings.

QUAKE A shaking or trembling sensation, often felt when opening the day's mail, which generally consists of bills or letters advising of the deaths of old friends. Also an earthquake, sometimes described as 'The Big One', an event awaited with some trepidation, particularly by Wellingtonians.

QUEEN The sovereign. A lady, much admired by the older generation, whose superhuman dignity allows her to ignore the antics of her somewhat dysfunctional family.

QUEEN MOTHER The mother of the sovereign, even more revered by the older generation. Younger people, who did not live through the war, are less impressed by the Queen Mother, being distracted by her taste for funny hats and gin.

QUILT A bed cover. Often handmade and regarded as

a family heirloom. Quilt-making has recently re-emerged as an art form, causing many ladies to buy stronger 'hobby glasses'.

QUIRK A gesture that is peculiar to an individual. Quirky behaviour varies considerably, and can range from the raising of an eyebrow at inappropriate behaviour to the growing of strange vegetables. As one ages one often develops more and more quirks, of which one is generally unaware until one's family points them out.

QUIT A word unknown to the elderly.

QUEEN MOTHER

RABBIT A burrowing animal. Once a staple part of the rural diet, now regarded as a virus-infected pest. Mention of rabbits tends to cause older listeners to assume a blank stare as their thoughts drift back to the exquisite taste and aroma of rabbit stew.

RACE A speed contest. Going to the races involved weeks of preparation for both humans and horses. The male race-goer dressed in his very best suit, with a trilby hat perched on his head at a rakish angle and a pair of binoculars draped loosely over one shoulder. A ticket dangling casually from a waistcoat button announced discreetly that he was a 'Member'. Ladies dressed in their most elegant finery, agonising for weeks over what hat to wear.

Non-members entered the course through separate gates, paying an entry fee and buying a race book. Non-members who 'lost their shirts' were forced to return home and try and convince their wives that the collar was worn out anyway. See NAG.

RADIO Once called the 'wireless'. The invention of the wireless opened up the world in a way that is now hard to imagine. Good and bad news, special events and sporting occasions could all be described to the previously uninformed public. Huddled around the wireless, the entire family would laugh at the antics of 'Dad and Dave', or thrill to 'Night Beat' and 'Doctor Paul', while mothers listened to the cleaning and cooking secrets of Aunt Daisy. These famous names have long-since faded away, to be replaced with Holmes (who?), Mark and Muzzy of 95 WM and Whiz Punk and Trash.

RAFFLE A lottery, common in clubs and at church fairs. Particularly popular with the older generation, who unhesitatingly subscribe to any raffle on offer.

RAZOR An instrument for the removal of facial hair. In the past the daily shave was performed with the 'safety razor', an instrument which removed any natural or unnatural projections or blemishes on the face. Blades

RAZOR

Redundant

came in small packets and could only be used once, although some hardy individuals attempted to maintain an edge by rubbing it in an arc inside a glass tumbler. These people were easily identified by the numerous pieces of tissue paper attached to their faces.

A 'cutthroat razor' was an item used by a barber, who wore a white coat and bore a striking resemblance to a dentist, although he generally charged much less. The 'cutthroat' inspired at least as much fear as a visit to the dentist, however.

REDUNDANT When your position in a working establishment is terminated. Once called 'getting the sack', today it means getting the sack.

REFUND Believed to be paid out by the Inland Revenue Department on rare occasions. Few people have ever met anyone who has received an IRD refund.

REMOTE A device for controlling the television set or similar appliances from a distance, enabling the user to change the settings at will, much to the annoyance of any other viewers present. The dominant male usually takes sole charge of the instrument, thus ensuring that the women are not able to view 'Coronation Street' or Royal weddings when there is an important sports programme on another channel.

REPEAT Generally associated with television, red peppers and cucumbers.

REPUBLIC A state presided over by a president, in New Zealand's case the suggestion being that such a person should replace the QUEEN. Few elderly people are in favour of this idea, preferring to retain the remaining ties between New Zealand and the 'Old Country', while many young people do not know who the queen is and so see no reason why she should head the country. The major stumbling block to New Zealand becoming a republic is the lack of any likely candidates for the position of president.

RESPECT Consideration for the feelings and property of others; feelings of esteem. In previous times respect was automatically paid to those who were older and had more experience; however, today respect is generally reserved for the young and/or the wealthy. The opposite is disrespect (see PARLIAMENT).

RETIREMENT See REDUNDANT.

RING The token of a betrothal. Some fortunate ladies actually receive rings that contain diamonds or other precious stones.

People, especially women, who have recently become engaged should be aware of the laboratory-made gems which sell at half the price of the genuine article. The giving of anything other than the genuine article should be looked on with disfavour, and serious consideration given to terminating the engagement, otherwise known as 'disengagement'.

The wedding ring symbolises a lifelong bond between

two individuals, but this item is becoming a rarity in today's society. See FIDELITY.

ROBUST Being in good health. Robust men often greet their friends with a slap on the shoulder, being quite unaware that the force of the slap has the potential to dislocate their less robust friends' joints, or send their noses into their beer glasses. As one ages, the term robust is less and less frequently applied.

ROUGE A red powder or cream that was once applied to the face as a cosmetic. It took considerable practice to control, and inexperienced ladies often appeared to be suffering from a fever, with extremely high cheek colour. Rouge was viewed with some suspicion by more genteel ladies (see HUSSY).

RUGBY The dominant religion of New Zealand.

S

SAUSAGE Skin-covered processed meat, also known as 'chorus girls', 'bangers' and 'mystery bags'. Once a staple part of the New Zealand diet, now a gourmet item which comes in a range of flavours. Caution is advised when faced with the curried and Mexican varieties.

SAVE To put aside surpluses for future use; for example, to save money so that one may lead a comfortable life in retirement. Many never achieve this goal, but with help from a benevolent government they survive. The search for such a government, however, presents a problem.

SAVELOY A red SAUSAGE, without which children's parties would not be the same, and rugby-club menus would be restricted to thickly sliced bread, mustard and tomato sauce.

SCALES Instruments used to ascertain weight. Used by only the most courageous elderly people, who invariably cast doubts on their accuracy.

SCANDAL A public disgrace or outrage. Scandals are generally spread by word of mouth, the listener looking

Scarf

SCALES

disapproving and pretending lack of interest before passing the story on to the next person they meet. Scandals often provide the highlight of an otherwise boring day. Some people class the President Clinton-Monica Lewinsky affair as a scandal, but it is better described as a farce.

SCARF An article of clothing worn round the neck. Males are restricted to white silk scarves, while women have a large range from which to choose. A lengthy ritual of former times, known as 'getting ready to go to town', culminated in selecting the correct scarf, after applying make-up, making sure stocking seams were straight, teasing and combing hair, and making sure shoes, handbag and gloves all matched and were in good order. Popular designs on scarves included flowers, animals, scenes of distant towns, and members of royalty; less often seen were All Blacks, wrestlers and male 'pin-ups'.

SCENT Now called perfume. The choice for respectable women used to be limited to 'Evening in Paris' (offering the fragrance of the working-class quarter) and lavender water. Today the choice is much wider, and perfumes have names that are aggressive or suggestive rather than romantic; for example, Red Door, Opium and Polo Sport.

SCHOOL A place of learning. Remembered fondly by most as a place where lifelong friendships were formed. In the old days the class was ruled over by the teacher, who drilled the 'three Rs' into their pupils, despite the pupils' best efforts to oppose the process. Most pupils left school able to read and write.

Today's schools teach sport. Uniforms are of the tracksuit variety, and assembly resembles a rehearsal for the Commonwealth Games. New English words, such as 'Wot!' 'Yeh!' and 'Cor!', are taught by teachers, who wear T-shirts, sandals and, in the case of the few males, beards, and spend a large part of their time striking for more pay so they can purchase protective clothing and study self-defence.

SCULLERY Formerly, the part of the house where the dishes were washed. This process took place after every meal, and took a considerable time, as plates, pots and pans were rubbed, scrubbed, scoured, rinsed, dried and

Seasonable

stored; at the same time there was inevitably an argument among the children about whose turn it was to dry, which frequently degenerated into fisticuffs and tears — hence the phrase, 'There'll be tears before bedtime'.

SEASONABLE Describes the foods and fashions of the season. Previously foods such as tomatoes, peas, lettuces, pears, apples and grapes were only available 'in season'; as a consequence they were much prized and eagerly awaited. Today, any food is available at any time of the year, and we fling packets of frozen foods into our supermarket trolleys without any feelings of anticipation or excitement. While this constant availability does not enhance flavour (remember your dad's peas?), it does tend to enhance price.

SECURITY A feeling of safety, once found at home. Now security requires sophisticated electronic 'systems' which include sirens, programmes, sensors, dogs, guards, beepers and high fences. Security lights which automatically illuminate an area in response to movement are a great help to an intruder, enabling them to make a quick escape from your property without incurring injury.

If one is feeling threatened, or insecure, one can dial the emergency number 111, which will result in one's call being placed on a waiting list, similar to the hospital waiting list. Getting on to the emergency short list requires murder, arson and other serious crimes. Burglary and assault on elderly ladies are not classified as serious.

Shroud

SENSE Senses make us aware of the world around us. Common sense is a learned attribute that is very common in the elderly but rare in the young. Other senses, however, such as taste, smell, hearing and sight, tend to decline with age. The only really essential sense is a sense of humour, which at least helps one to cope with the loss of the other senses.

SERMON The part of a church service when older males take a NAP.

SHOE An article of clothing worn on the foot. Once made from the finest kid leather, which required frequent cleaning and polishing. Today we wear sports shoes, which are colourful, comfortable and can be thrown in the washing machine to be cleaned. Women's shoes used to include high-heeled shoes, or stilettos, which were useful for defending one's honour but had a long-term effect on the feet similar to that of foot binding.

SHOUT To make a loud noise. Also to pay for drinks. Some men deliberately shout a lot before entering a bar, so that when they shout the drinks they are not heard. This is a tricky practice as one's friends usually catch on very quickly and have their own means of exacting revenge.

SHROUD The last new garment you will ever own, and one you won't have chosen, tried on or even held up in front of a shop mirror.

Skip

SKIP To leap over a rope. A girls' pastime that is usually accompanied by sung verses, the words of which may be many years old. Today skipping has largely been replaced by virtual pets, electronic toys that are made in Japan and make beeping noises.

SLENDER Slim, lithe, willowy ... remember?

SLOBBER A vulgar term used to describe an affectionate KISS. Used by the wife of a man to whom she has been married for more than thirty years.

SMACK Formerly an act performed to indicate to a CHILD that you were displeased with their behaviour. Today such actions result in prosecution and a five-year prison sentence. Also a type of KISS (see also SLOBBER).

SMOKE The residue from a burning substance. Smoking was once a popular, indeed glamorous, pastime, but it is now considered an antisocial act, and smokers are no longer welcome in offices, restaurants or most homes. Wives have always known the evils of smoking, which include burning up money and imparting a disgusting smell to one's wardrobe.

SNOB A person who fails to acknowledge you as they drive past in their new car at a speed of 120 kph. To your wife, it is the lady across the road who has just had new carpet and curtains fitted.

SNUFF Powdered tobacco, which was sniffed up the

nose, heaven knows why! Also a slang term meaning to die, although the connection between the two has not been proven.

SOCIALITE A person who may or may not own wealth, but is always in possession of an Oxford accent. A 'cellulite' is a person who is a socialite but has served a prison sentence.

SOLICITOR A legal adviser, whose bill for making out your will makes a severe dent in the value of your estate. Also one who solicits.

SOUP A tasty and nutritious liquid food that MOTHERS used to be able to create out of nothing. Traditionally soup contained bones, vegetable odds and ends, and other ingredients which were best known only to the creator. Today soup generally comes from a packet or a can, although restaurants have been known to make their own soups, using strange ingredients such as lettuce and avocadoes.

SPONGE A light, fluffy cake eaten at afternoon tea time. It is best filled with whipped cream and homemade jam, and served as a thick wedge on the best china. Sponge-making was one of the defining skills of the accomplished housewife, and the competition among women to make the lightest, highest cake was always fierce, although often carefully concealed.

SPORT A form of recreation involving strenuous exercise.

Stain

Some young ladies used to be labelled 'good sports', although they had probably never played tennis, rugby or any other sport.

STAIN A coloured patch that suddenly appears on one's clothing, usually caused by spilling food or drink. Stains almost always appear when you are wearing your best suit, and the spillage will always be one of red wine or food containing tomato paste. They invariably occur at parties to which all your most important friends and family members have been invited. The only way to deal with stains is to ignore them until your guests have departed, then hand the article of clothing over to your wife to deal with as soon as she has finished the dishes.

STARCH A substance for stiffening clothes, the aim being to make them as uncomfortable as humanly possible. One of the few improvements of modern life is that starch is no longer used.

STOUT A polite word for fat.

STRIKE To withdraw one's labour as a protest against pay or working conditions. Strikes are now rare, the introduction of the Employment Contracts Act having made all employees completely satisfied with their working environment.

STUD
1. An infuriatingly small fastener, used to attach the collar to a shirt;

2. A male person with a vastly inflated ego regarding his success with the ladies. Caution is advised.

SUIT An essential part of the male wardrobe, the choice of which is always supervised by the lady of the house. Suits are only worn on the most important occasions, and tend to remain in the wardrobe for long periods, covered with the plastic bag supplied following the necessary drycleaning after the previous wearing (see STAIN).

Some people, such as lawyers, members of the clergy, mortgage consultants and stockbrokers, wear suits every day, the suit being similar to a company logo and enabling them to be recognised as 'professionals'.

SUPERANNUITANT A person who has paid taxes all their working life and has played no small part in the development of the country. Hospitals, libraries, schools, roads, bridges, tunnels, railways and numerous other essential facilities were developed and paid for by today's superannuitants, who are rewarded with constant complaints by those in power about the cost to current taxpayers of maintaining any sort of superannuation scheme. Such appreciation is most gratifying. (Note: the war is not mentioned, as this provokes accusations of self-pity, as well as reminding politicians of the photo opportunities provided by memorial services and old servicemen.)

SWEAR To use profane language; for example, damn! blast! hell! rats! and strewth! Such words were never within the vocabulary of a LADY or GENTLEMAN.

T

TABLE The table (that is, the kitchen table) used to be the family meeting place. It had many uses, including providing a place to eat, read, sew and play games, as well as prepare food. It was also the place where serious family discussions took place, homework was done and accounts were pored over.

Today the kitchen table has more or less fallen into disuse, as meals, bought in packets from supermarkets or takeaway bars, are eaten sitting in front of the television set, and there is no such thing as a family discussion. Any homework is done either on the floor or at the computer.

TACT Saying the right thing at the right time. Extreme tact is advised when filing a claim with an insurance company, speaking to a police constable regarding one's driving ability, communicating with a government department, and meeting or staying with one's wife's/husband's family. This last is particularly hazardous, and generally by the time one has developed the tact necessary to deal with the situation it is too late and irreparable damage has been done.

Taste

TALK Verbal communication. A dying art among the young, who appear to have regressed to the primitive grunts of prehistory. Accomplished talkers are in great demand, often becoming entertainers and commanding high fees. Poor talkers tend to write down their thoughts rather than speak them, and this may lead them to compile such things as dictionaries.

TAP A device through which water is supplied. Early taps were attached to tanks, and only delivered cold water. Hot water, essential for the male shaving ritual and for making tea, was obtained by boiling a KETTLE. Hot-water taps are a luxury only really appreciated by those who grew up before they were invented, and a few trampers and outdoor adventurers. Many elderly people still take great delight in the fact that they can now take a bath whenever the fancy takes them, rather than planning hours ahead. (Of course, they may need to make sure there is someone about to help them in and out of the bath, but that's a different story — see AGILE.)

TASTE Personal preference. Tastes change dramatically over the years, particularly tastes in clothing, houses, cars, entertainment and food. What is considered 'tasteful' to one generation is often considered laughable to the generation that precedes or follows it, but the observant will notice that it is not long before the cycle turns and the truly old-fashioned becomes fashionable again. This is possibly the reason why many young people get on better with their grandparents than with their parents, and vice versa.

Tea

TEA A wonderful beverage, without which this country would have remained undeveloped. Tea is used to soothe the angry, comfort the bereaved, refresh the tired and warm the cold. Today there is a huge range of 'herbal' teas, which may be useful for curing headaches and soothing women's complaints, but it is hard to imagine them being taken up by road gangs and sheep shearers.

TELEPHONE A mixed blessing as a means of communication, the telephone conversation takes precedence over every other form of talking, but also enables us to keep in touch with family and friends wherever they are. It is hard to say whether the tyranny of the telephone has increased or reduced in recent years, with the invention of the answering machine, pager, cordless phone, car phone and mobile phone. The last of these is perhaps the most loved and hated of all, providing business people who cannot afford offices to make and receive phone calls in public streets and lavatories and on park benches, while no longer can errant husbands use the excuse that they couldn't call home because there wasn't a phone.

TETCHY A condition common to us all, particularly when we are tired, anxious or feeling defensive. See also NAG.

TIP A place for putting rubbish. Once a large hole in the ground, now a multi-million-dollar concrete extravaganza, staffed by people in multi-coloured uniforms who drive large machines. The rubbish disappears each day

Tradition

when it is taken to a large hole in the ground. In reality, only the dump charges are new.

TONIC A pick-me-up. Many elderly people will remember the ominous words, 'What you need is a tonic,' which were followed by the emergence of a large bottle containing a highly coloured and foul-tasting liquid. Many still rely on a tonic to pick them up at the end of the day, but the highly coloured liquid of the past has been replaced by a clear fluid that is mixed with another clear fluid known as gin (see QUEEN MOTHER).

TRADITION Customs and behaviour passed on from generation to generation. The British have many traditions, while New Zealanders are still in the process of

TONIC

forming their own unique customs. Among these are the stag party, rugby, refusing to drink imported beer (a small quantity of Australian is acceptable), Marmite sandwiches and, for the young (or not so young), Weetbix. For some reason all these examples are rather less flamboyant than trooping the colour. Some traditions have proved short-lived, such as 'Ladies a Plate, Please.'

TRAM A mode of transport that is now obsolete. Trams were exciting and romantic vehicles, and boarding and descending from them sharpened passengers' senses as they avoided stepping on the lines and into the traffic.

TREACLE A sweet, sticky substance which was often mixed with sulphur and taken medicinally by loudly protesting children. Now replaced by golden syrup (cockies' joy), which is delicious on hot-buttered scones. Calorie caution!

TUB A large sink; often found in pairs (see MANGLE). A tub was used for washing newly dug vegetables, rinsing out woollen clothing, hand-washing, baby-bathing, and washing small dogs — preferably not at the same time.

U

UPBRINGING The social and moral standards learned from our parents. In the past upbringing involved being fortified by the RAZOR strop, bed without tea, withdrawal of motherly services and temporary banishment from the family. Today upbringing works on a reward system; for example, 'If you continue to act in this manner, you won't get the Sanshiba Automatic Banger Stereo, Complete with Mind Destroying Noise, for your birthday.' Most homes are now without razor strops, these having been replaced by fourteen-head close-shaving cordless razors, which are absolutely useless for the chastisement of children, thereby failing to carry out one of the essential functions of razors.

USEFUL To be of service. Many retired people feel they are no longer useful, and their offspring frequently agree, until for some reason babysitting, dishwashing, mending, sewing and money-lending services are withdrawn.

USEFUL

V

VALENTINE One's sweetheart; the one you send flowers and cards to on Valentine's Day. Many married couples exchange such tokens, as do the young, many of whom send, and receive, a number of them (often, in fact, sending them to themselves, in the horrid fear that no-one else will).

VEIL A covering for the face which creates a great air of mystery. Many veils are diaphanous, thus scarcely impairing the wearer's vision. Some wedding veils are made from heavier materials, however, and completely hide the identity of the wearer until after the ceremony. This can cause great distress when the groom lifts the veil to kiss the bride, only to find that he has married the extremely plain daughter of his parents' next-door neighbours, instead of his true love from Pahiatua. Extreme caution is advised.

VENUS The goddess of love and desire, who it is not appropriate to describe in this dictionary. Also a planet, an acceptable subject, as star-gazing is an approved hobby of the elderly.

Veteran

VETERAN

VETERAN An old serviceman or woman, or an old car. Both have rallies, although veteran car rallies are much less noisy and boisterous than the other sort.

VICE
1. Used by urban police to form squads.
2. (Also vise.) An indispensable tool, found bolted to the workbench and used for gripping objects with even greater tenacity than a sticky toffee adheres to a set of dentures.

There are other meanings for this word, but I can't remember what they are.

VIRILE Youthful, active and potent. Potent drugs are now available for the continuation of virility far beyond the norm. The effects of these drugs may be compared to replacing a standard Mini motor with a supercharged V8. Problems may arise because the gearbox, transmission and steering are badly worn, and a complete overhaul may be necessary. Elderly human knees and hips are especially vulnerable to excess stress, and caution is advised.

W

WAIST

WAIST The measurement around the middle of the body; increasingly difficult to find as one gets older, and less important.

WAR A dreadful event during which normal, pleasant people are trained to kill other people, without the two ever having met. War leaves a feeling of unreality. The wounds last a lifetime.

Wine

WATCH A device for telling the time. Formerly a pocket watch, complete with chain, was hung over the lower chest. At appropriate moments it would be flamboyantly withdrawn from the waistcoat pocket and a lever pressed, exposing the face. It was an engineering marvel which always showed the correct time. Today the pocket watch has been replaced by the wristwatch which has no style at all, is driven by batteries and frequently plays a tune. The worst sorts 'bleep' at inappropriate times, such as in the most moving moments of a concert, or just when you have dropped off to sleep (sometimes the same thing).

WEATHER The vagaries of the elements. Forecasting the weather is a highly technical science, the results of which are brought to us by 'presenters'. These are often failed comedians who bombard us with forecasts and predictions using charts, numbers and arrows, none of which they, or we, understand. The most reliable part of a weather 'forecast' is what the weather did yesterday, but even this is subject to debate. Listening to the weather forecast on the wireless used to be an essential part of the farmer's day, but few farmers now bother, as they have heard all the jokes before.

WINE The fermented juice of the grape. Previously only available in half-gallon bottles, with the choice being limited to three types of sherry and one type of port. Today the choice is bewildering and enough to make the serious drinker stay with beer.

Wisdom

WISDOM Something that comes with the job . . . of being a full-time elderly person.

WRINKLE A fold in the skin, correctly attributed to the shrinking of the internal body. Wrinkles can be cured by eating far too much, and total smoothness can be achieved by eating fish and chips five times a week. Ask your doctor for a prescription.

X

XYLOPHONE

XYLOPHONE A noisy and infuriating toy that is frequently given to young grandchildren by grandparents in retaliation for the irritating habits of their parents. Fortunately, easily destroyed by being accidentally stamped on just as you are leaving the house.

Y

YARN

YARN A spun thread for knitting. Also a tall story. Some yarns do relate true experiences, while others have no basis in truth. Most wives can immediately spot the difference.

YEAR A period of time. When young, it lasts forever. When old, it seems to last a day.

YES Affirmative. A small word which can cause the utterer much anguish in the future. Great caution is advised.

YOUNG The opposite of OLD. Attractive, fashionable, desirable. In the aged, feeling young can lead to slipped discs, twisted knees, breathlessness and indigestion.

Z

ZERO The score you would obtain if you were foolish enough to enter the Miss or Mister Universe contest.

ZODIAC Your future in the stars. To be consulted before making any plans for the day. A warning. Read only one publication, as advice seems to vary, which can cause disorientation and embarrassment.

ZZZ The most pleasant and peaceful of sensations, generally indulged in after the family have gone home, after a good meal, in fact after any exertion at all. See NAP.